Siena
City of Art

The Castles of Chianti

Plan of the City
220 Photo in colour
Map of the Chianti country

Distributore esclusivo
TURBANTI FABIO
Via Sicilia 1 - Tel. 0577 - 51260
SIENA

Published and printed by

Narni - Terni
ITALIA

Siena, City of Art

The tourist who goes along the modern road leading to Siena from Florence, sees all around himself a very pleasant landscape, rich in green fields of olive-trees, vineyards and cypresses. The medieval and characteristic towers of S. Gemignano rising on the right side, near Poggibonsi, tell us that Siena is near. The lanscape looks quite different to those who reach the town through the south of the province by the Cassia or Valdichiana roads. This side of the country, though bare in some of its parts, presents characteristic and suggestive features, thanks mainly to its picturesque clays and hills of clay with their corn-fields. On top of these hills there is always a tree, as if it were a sort of plume.

Siena was a Roman colony during the Republican age. During the imperial age and the early Middle ages, it went through many terrible events. Its expansion, however, was always limited by the greater power and rivalry of Florence. Being far from the sea and open only towards the lands of the Maremma, Siena was often besieged and devastated and had to face civil wars and terrible pestilences.

After the domination of the Longobards and Franks, it passed under the Bishop-Counts, towards the middle of the XIth century. Then there was the turn of the Consuls, with a lay government. And it was in this period that Siena reached the height of its political and economic power, specially after the famous battle of Montaperti in 1260, by which it defeated the Florentines. Arts and culture flourished in this time. Thanks mainly to the Government of the Nine, which, restored in 1277, ruled for about 70 years, the magnificents monuments of Siena were built during this period of time. The renowned « Piazza del Campo » is its most precious pearl and the centre of its peculiar town-planning. This square, with its famous buildings, is the spacious and resounding shell, where the city-life takes place. It is the suggestive amphitheatre, whose background is constituted only by the « Palazzo Pubblico » with the Tower of Mangia, the best example of the 14th century civil architecture. The characteristic medieval look of Siena dates back to the same century. The town has kept its original look. In its streets made of bricks and stones, among the high buildings, adorned with elegant three-mullioned windows and slender ogive arches, in the suggestive courtyards, in the closed and dark entrance halls, in the narrow alleys and squares, you perceive a sort of ancient atmosphere, which makes Siena so charming.

It is a medieval town, but mostly a town of art. If one is intensely excited at the sight of the Campo, one is amazed at the sight of the monuments of the town, the Cathedral and the other churches, the museums. Everywhere one finds precious masterpieces, wonderful works of Nicola and Giovanni Pisano, Duccio and Simone Martini, Donatello and Ghiberti, who have left here some examples of their immortal art.

Painting, which was the most genuine and significant expression of the creativeness of the Sienese, new architectonic ideas and an original school of sculpture, one of the best in Italy, more refined technics in gold working and designs, made of Siena one of the greatest leader in the field of art in Italy and Europe, since the end of the 13th century and the early 14th century. If in the 14th century the Sienese art reached its height with Duccio and Simone Martini, Pietro and Ambrogio Lorenzetti, we must not forget that during the two next centuries the figurative arts reached very high levels, thanks to artists like Jacopo della Quercia, Sassetta, Sano di Pietro, Giovanni di Paolo, just to mention a few. When in the 17th century the Town of Siena declined because of internal divisions and the decreasing richness of its merchants and bankers and so was overcome by the rising power of Florence and annexed to the Grand Duchy of Tuscany, its people took refuge, as it were, in the glories of the past, in its institutions and greatest memories.

Being conscious of having a personality of their own, the Sienese people kept its love for the old districts, its civil and religious traditions, the Palio, which is something more than a horse-race. The Palio is a wonderful show commemorating the glory of the ancient Republic. It is a popular feast, which, since the Middle Ages, aroused people's enthusiasm. By the Palio, the Sienese express the feelings and passions of their 17 « contrade » or districts. And it is by this fight among the contrade that the ancient Siena goes on living together with the actual Siena, in the harmonious and suggestive atmosphere of a historical and artistic environment, which is unique in the world.

The Cathedral and the Palazzo Pubblico

The peculiar shape of Piazza del Campo or simply « il Campo » (the Field) is due to the canalization and diversion of rain-waters on an irregular and bare ground, shaped like an amphitheatre, where the three hills, on which Siena rises, meet together. This happened during the 13th century. This square, however, is incomparably beautiful and the essential element of the Sienese town-planning. It is famous all over the world and unique in its kind. It looks like a shell, which shows the particular nature of the ground, harmonizing nature and art. It is paved along its borders, while the central part is made of bricks arranged like a fish-bone and divided into nine parts by white stone-strips, which commemorate the Rule of the Nine. At the base of the shell, as a sort of background on the wide cavea of the square, there is the Palazzo Pubblico (Public Palace), surrounded by remarkable buildings, with the slender Tower of Mangia, and, at its foot, the Cappella di Piazza (the Chapel of the Square). It is magnificent and elegant, simple and picturesque at the same time, in its structure and harmonious division of its area. It is the most renowned one of the Gothic-Tuscan buildings and the best example of the Sienese civil architecture, which, more than others, presents more slender lines and a peculiar ornate style.

The history of this building is strictly connected with the political and economical affairs of Siena. It was begun in 1250, as records of that time show. In 1299 the central part was completed, while the building of the two wings was begun in 1305. In 1310 the Palazzo had the shape which it kept till in 1680 and at the beginning of the 18th century some other parts were added to its structure, though the stylistic unity of its front was kept. The front is made of stone in its lower part with the characteristics Sienese arches. The second and third storeys are made of bricks, with two orders of three-mullioned windows. A fourth storey, higher than the two side bodies, with small arches and merlons. Among the mullioned windows of this storey there is a large copper disk with the monogram of Christ, the symbol of St. Bernardine, and on the sides two stony she-wolves. The Palazzo Pubblico was once the seat of the Government and the Mayor of the ancient Sienese Republic. Today it is the seat of the Municipality.

Palazzo Pubblico

The Fonte Gaia

FONTE GAIA – This fountain was built on the opposite side of the Palazzo Pubblico, where once a 14th century fountain was. It was made by Jacopo di Pietro, called « della Quercia », probably after Quercegrossa, his family's place, around Siena. This fountain is shaped like a rectangular basin, surrounded, on three sides, by a high parapet. It was made between 1409 and 1419. It looks like 'a magnificent altar made of white marbles, which anticipates some of the basic features of the Renaissance, with its strict connection between sculpture and architecture and plastic forms. Among the sculptures adorning the fountain in the centre, there is the image of the Madonna, surrounded by the Virtues and the Creation of Adam and Adam and Eve driven out of Eden. In 1858 the original reliefs were substituted with reproductions made by Tito Sarocchi and transferred into the Loggia of the Palazzo Pubblico.

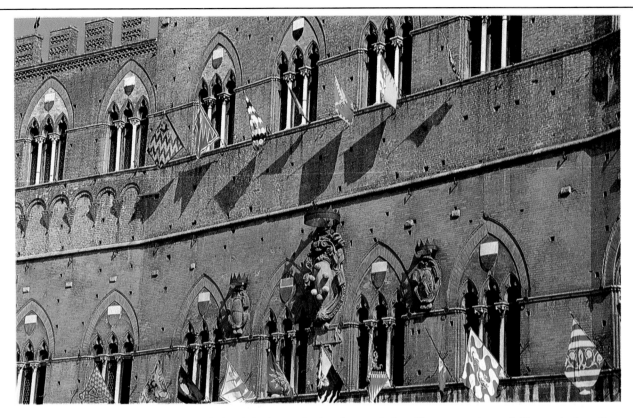

PALAZZO PUBBLICO – a detail of the facade, with the flags of the 17 « contrade » of Siena during the Palio.

PALAZZO SANSEDONI – surmounted by a rhomb-shaped tower, this building, erected in the former part of the 13th century and enlarged in 1399, presents the same basic features of the Palazzo Pubblico, as other buildings of the Campo.

The Piazza del Campo and Palazzo Pubblico

The Cappella di Piazza and Torre del Mangia

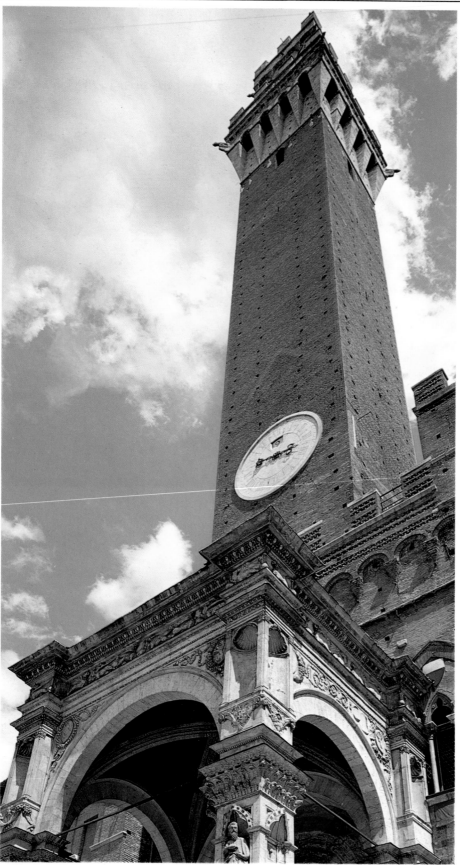

CAPPELLA DI PIAZZA - This Chapel, surmounted by the Tower of Mangia, was built to fulfill a vow made by the Sienese during the 1348 pestilence. It was begun in 1352 by Domenico d'Agostino and completed around 1376 by Giovanni di Cecco who completed also the pillars and the roof.

THE TOWER OF MANGIA, seen from the Mayor's Courtyard. This slender tower, dominating the town, shows not only the architectonic genius but of the workers of that time but is also a great work of engineering. It is called so after Giovanni di Duccio, named "Mangiaguadagni" o more simply "Mangia", engaged by the Municipality to ring the bells. The automaton, which was put there to strike the hours on the tower till 1780, was called "Mangia". The brick pipe was erected by the Aretine brothers Minuccio di Rinaldo and Francesco Naldi, under the direction of Giovanni d'Agostino (1338-1348).

After a very slender cornice, there is the first travertine coping, with two coat-of-arms of the Municipality, with a rampant lion in the middle, then the bell-tower made on designs of Lippo Memmi (1341). Above it there is the big bell cast in 1665 and called by the Sienese "Campanone" or "Sunto", because it was "christened" Maria Assunta.

The characteristic roofs of Siena and the Piazza del Campo

Courtyard of the Palazzo Pubblico

PALAZZO PUBBLICO – « The Mayor's Courtyard » – One reaches it by a door near the Cappella di Piazza. It was built in 1325 and restored in 1929. It consists of a portico surmounted by a storey with a series of large three-mullioned windows. Along the walls there are some coat-of-arms of Mayors and a fresco, badly damaged and incomplete, dating back to the 14th century and representing the Madonna and two angels. In the photo: the remains of the statue of « Mangia » and « The She-wolf feeding the twins », a golden tin work of Giovanni di Turino (1429-30), which are in the vestibule and at the end of the portico.

The panorama from the Tower of the Palazzo Pubblico

The top of the tower is 88 metres high up to the last merlons and 102 up to the point of the lightning-conductor. One reaches it through the Mayor's Courtyard. From there one can enjoy a wonderful view on the whole town and the surrounding hills. Towards south-east (above, on the left) one can see the Basilica of S. Maria dei Servi, and, on the horizon, Mount Amiata. On a side one can see a corner of Piazza del Campo with Palazzo Sansedoni and, below, another sight of the town with the apse of the Cathedral, the belfry and the walls of the New Cathedral.

Piazza del Campo on a pleasant Spring morning: the shadows of the Palazzo Pubblico and the Tower of Mangia on the square and the nearby buildings suggestively reproduce the silhouette of the most famous Sienese building. It is famous because it is beautiful and represents the architectonic unity of the square. This building, however, is not connected with the square only from the artistic, but also historical, traditional and cultural points of view.

It was here that the Sienese, through the centuries, have faced the most important events of their history; it was here that they have rejoiced and suffered. If the Campo is the heart of Siena, the scenery of its past history and centre of its life, the Palazzo is the symbol of that history, the guardian of its dearest memories and cultural values. The noblest feelings of the people of Siena go on living in this square, which is the most important testimony of the extraordinary artistic and cultural development during the age of the Free Towns.

PALAZZO PUBBLICO - Interior - The Sala del Mappamondo
The large council hall known as the Sala del Mappamondo (from a map painted by Ambrogio Lorenzetti in the 14th century and now lost) is situated on the first floor of the Palazzo Pubblico, whose rooms are now laid out as a Civic Museum. On the end walls are the two great frescoes of the Maestà and Guidoriccio da Fogliano by Simone Martini. This latter fresco, as we will explain below, has become the symbol of the civic and military power of the glorious Republic of Siena. In recent years, during a restoration carried out under the direction of the Superintendent of Artistic and Cultural Properties Piero Torriti, another significant fresco came to light in its lower part: it depicts a Castle and a Church with two personages in the foreground; undoubtedly antecedent in date to Simone Martini's fresco, it has plausibly been attributed to Duccio di Buoninsegna (c. 1314-15).
Below, a view of the hall with the "Maestà" in the background. This is the first work which can be securely attributed to Simone Martini. This artist was one of the greatest representatives of 14th century painting. If, according to Vasari, he died in 1344, when he was 60, it means that he was born in 1284. Simone painted the "Maestà" in 1315. Six years after, however, he had to restore the fresco because it was damaged by damp. Under a canopy supported by eight apostles, the Madonna and Child enthroned is surrounded by angels, saints and other apostles. A wide strip of 20 medallions with images of Christ, prophets and evangelists surrounds the composition. Below, in the centre, we see a double-faced figure representing the old and new laws and a medallion reproducing the seal of the Republic.

Guidoriccio da Fogliano, fresco by Simone Martini

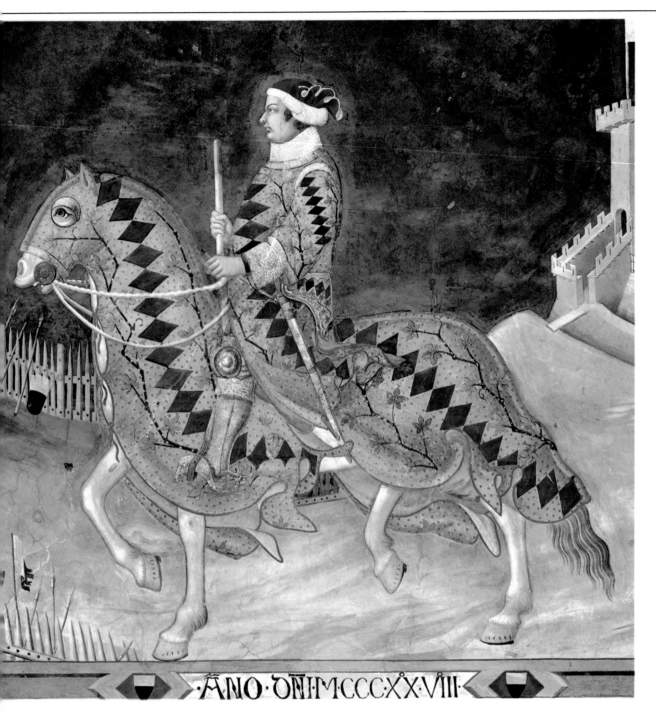

ĀNO·DŃI·MCCC·XX·VIII

THE GLOBE'S HALL – « Guidoriccio da Fogliano ». On the opposite side, above, there is another fresco of Simone Martini, representing « Guidoriccio da Fogliano » after the victory over the Castles of Montemassi and Sassoforte of Maremma, which had rebelled in Siena in 1328. The work, completed in 1329, was a part of a series of representations of Castles conquered by the Sienese Republic. Unfortunately this work went lost. In the centre, the « condottiero » (leader), magnificentely paraded, proud and silent, triumphally going towards the conquered castles. This fresco is certainly one of the best and most famous works of Simone Martini. The vast scene presents a sort of monumental magnificence, with the towered castles on the background. It is really a poetic and heroic evocation of the event.

The Maestà, fresco by Simone Martini

THE GLOBE'S HALL – A detail of the « Maestà ». It is considered the oldest fresco of the all Sienese painting. In this work Simone Martini combines the refined « French Gothic » style with Hellenistic elements taken from Duccio and new elements of the Italian art, represented by the Pisan sculptors and Giotto. The intense expressions of the characters, the delicate lines, the vivid volours, the refined details, all take you into another mystical reality.

In the pictures on this page: above, from left, a detail of the Virgin and Magdalen; below, S. Ansano and S. Crescenzio, who together with S. Vittore and Savino are the Patron Saints of Siena.

THE HALL OF PEACE or THE NINE – This hall is so called because it was the seat of the Government of the Nine. In it is kept the most famous cycle of secular frescoes of all the Sienese painting. It is one of the works of Ambrogio Lorenzetti of Siena (1319-1348), painted between 1337 and 1339.
The great political, didactic and moral representation consists of three parts: « The Allegory of the Good Government », which can be seen in the photo above; « The Results of the Good Government in the town and countryside », and « The Allegory and the Results of the Bad Government », below, all forming one composition. Unfortunately the latter one is badly damaged.

and Effects of Bad Government, by Ambrogio Lorenzetti

THE HALL OF PEACE OR THE NINE – « The Good Government » (a detail). « The Good Government » is represented by an old, solemn king dressed in white and black. These are the colours of the « Balzana », the Sienese flag, and the coat-of-arms of the town. On his left side, Justice, Temperance and Magnanimity; on his right side, Prudence, Fortitude and Peace. Above, the three theological virtues, while at the feet of the King the She-wolf feeds Aschius and Senius, sons of Remus and mythical founders of Siena. Below, « The Results of the Good Gouvernment in the town » (a detail): a view of the 14ht century Siena where, among towers and embattled buildings, various activities flourish, with elegant cavalcades along its streets, young dancers crowding the squares and streets of the town. Here are the harmoniously combined features of a society, which is happy thanks to the great virtues of the « Good Gouvernment ».

THE HALL OF PEACE – Another detail of the Results of the Good Gouvernment: a door on the city walls opens on to the countryside, where life pulses among farm-houses, castles, vineyards, woods and olive-groves. In the side picture: the dancers.

This is the most lively and interesting composition of the whole cycle. Lorenzetti describes here every-day life – the market, a cavalcade outside the gates, a lady dressed in red on a white horse, dancing girls. Each event, however, and each figure bear witness to the 14th century way of life and its deep and genuine values. It is so that the imposing conceptual and allegorical structure, based on the contrast between good and evil, the good and bad government, becomes poetry by a very original language.

And it is in this work that Ambrogio Lorenzetti reached his artistic ideal, which expresses itself in the perfect balance of all the values, between colour and volume, in the lines clearly marking mass and colour.

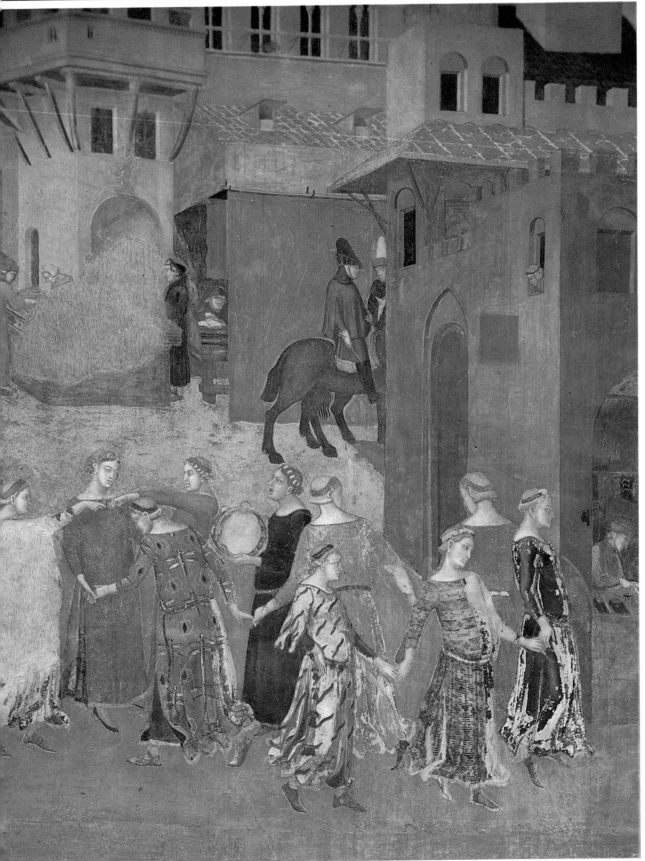

Chapel of the Palazzo Pubblico

THE CHAPEL — Near the Globe's Hall there is a magnificent chapel, closed by an elegant wrought-iron gate, designed probably by Jacopo della Quercia and made in 1437 by the Sienese Giacomo di Vita and his son Giovanni. Above the marble altar of Marrina, there is a beautiful painting of Sodoma representing the « Holy Family and St. Leonard. On the vaults of the walls of the chapel there are frescoes made by Taddeo di Bartolo around 1407 and representing the Evangelists, the Doctors of the Church, various prophets and stories of the Virgin's life. Below, the funeral of the Madonna.

Along the walls of the chapel one can admire a precious wooden choir with 21 stalls, all carved, with carved panels on their backs, illustrating the articles of the Creed. It is one of the works of Domenico di Niccolò, who, having made this choir, was called « Domenico dei Cori ». This choir, made between 1415 and 1428, is a real masterpiece of woodworking art, thanks to its harmonious structure and elegant decorations.

The Choir

Naval Battle between the Venetians and the Imperial Force

« BALIA » HALL – This hall, divided into two sections by an arch, is so called after the College of the Judges of « Balia » (power), which used to hold its meetings in this very place. It is full of frescoes. The vaults, up to the cornices, were frescoed in 1407-1408 by the Sienese painter Martino di Bartolomeo, who divided the ceiling into triangular sections. In each section there is represented a Virtue. These Virtues are elegant feminine figures, which remind us of the painting of Ambrogio Lorenzetti. It is probably the best work of Martino di Bartolomeo. On the arch crossing the hall there are the figures of the Four Evangelists and six busts of emperors and warriors, while on the pillars there are other minor figures of Virtues. On the walls and lunettes above the arch there is a large cycle of frescoes made in 1408 by Spinello di Luca of Arezzo, called the Aretine (1346-1410). They represent the exploits of the pope Alexander III, belonging to the Sienese Bandinelli family, life and soul of the Lombard League and victor over Frederick Redbeard. This is one of the rare examples of the activity of a non-Sienese painter in Siena. Aretine, however, was well known in the town, because since 1404 he had been called by Sir Caterino di Corsino to paint in the Cathedral. These frescoes represent the last important work of this artist, who as helped by his son Parri, who was twenty at that time. They belong to the long 14th century tradition, dominated by the personality and activity of Giotto.

From the Balìa Hall, by a staircase, one can climb up to the large Loggia, open on four pillars, where the remains of Fonte Gaia, made by the Sienese Jacopo della Quercia, are kept. In the photo below, a corner of the hall; on the side plate, a detail of the oarsmen in « The naval battle between the Venetians and the Imperial forces at Punta Salvore », by Spinello Aretino.

The Sala dei Pilastri

THE PILLARS HALL — The two precious partitions of predella representing « St. Bernardine preaching in a field », in the photo above, and « The miracolours deliverance of Genuzia from the devil during the funeral of St. Bernardine », were brought in the Palazzo Pubblico from the Gallery of the Academy during early 19th century. Now they are in the Pillars Hall which is in front of that of Peace. They were made by Neroccio di Bartolomeo Landi (1447-1500) and probably date back to the artist's young years. We do not know when the predella was made, but we get some indication from the first panel, where is represented the front of the Palazzo Pubblico with the Chapel, without the later additions made by Federeghi in 1468.

The Cathedral

The history of this building is long and complicate. Though it is one of the most known and magnificent cathedrals in Europe, we know little about the period and circumstances of its foundation. The first sure testimony dates back to 1136, when a special deputation of citizens was entrusted with the building of the Cathedral. Then it passed under the administration of the monks of San Galgano's Abbey, till 1314. In 1284 Giovanni Pisano built only the lower part of the facade. In the mean time the building was completed with its three aisles, dome and belfry. During the early 14th century, however, the Sienese, at the height of their prosperity and power, thought to erect a new magnificent building to be added perpendicularly to the south-east side of the cathedral. So the building of the New Cathedral began. Lando di Pietra was first entrusted with the works, then Giovanni d'Agostino. In 1348, however, because of a pestilence and the instability of the building, the works stopped and a few years later the project was put aside. The unsafe parts were demolished, while some of the perimetrical front walls, the left side aisle and the walls of the facade, the so called « facciatone » dominating the town, were left standing. So the building of the old Cathedral went on. In 1382 the apse was completed, the middle aisle was made higher and the upper part of the facade was erected by Giovanni di Cecco. Though various interruptions and time have left their signs in the planning structures and decorations of the Cathedral, this wonderful marble building presents an extraordinary unity, from the rich marble facade, with its splendid mosaics, to the more simple but elegant sides and pointed high tower with white and black strips and a series of mullioned windows. This unity is due to the original and wonderful balance between the Gothic elements, more evident on the outside, and Romanesque elements of the interior. The facade is one of the masterpieces of the Italian art. Its lower part, Romanesque, made by Giovanni Pisano, is characterized by three large portals and elegant statues made also by Pisano, here substituted with copies to prevent them to be damaged, while the originals are kept in the nearby museum. The upper part is of Gothic style, three-pointed and with a very rich decoration.

Other views of the Cathedral

In the photos: The upper part of the central portal of the Cathedral flanked by clustered colonnettes adorned with a beautiful sculptured decoration of classical type comprising acanthus scrolls, putti and animal motifs, the work of Giovanni Pisano. In the architrave is a bas-relief by Tino di Camaino (c. 1285-1337) representing St. Joachim and St. Anna.

The modern bronze door (1958) is the work of the sculptor Enrico Manfrini and represents the glorification of the Virgin by God and by men.

In the upper part of the façade is a large rose window, surrounded by busts of patriarchs and prophets, and with statues of the Virgin (on top) and the four Evangelists (in the corners) all copies of the 14th century originals which are now preserved in the Cathedral Museum. The three triangular pediments are decorated with mosaics by Augusto Castellani (1877); the central one is surmounted by the statue of an angel by Tommaso Redi (1639).

The column surmounted by the wolf and the elegant windows of the 18th century Archbishop's Palace annexed to the left side of the Cathedral

To the side: a fine view of the Cathedral from a novel perspective in which the monument seems to rise from the roofs of the houses flanking the many alleyways in the city's historic centre.

The Cathedral: interior

ALBERTI·D·FRANCISCI·DE·ARINGHERIIS·EQUITIS·HYEROSOLIMITAN·

INTERIOR — The Latin cross shaped interior of the Cathedral has three aisles.

It is austere and magnificent at the same time, with its play of light and shade on the marbles covering, with white and black stripes, walls and pillars. Here colour dominates. There is suggestive contrast between the vertical pillars and the horizontal decorative stripes. This gives special prominence to the Sienese picturesque fantasy and refined sense of colour. All along the nave runs a cornice, supported by 172 busts of popes, a work dating back to 15th-16th century. Below, there are the busts of 36 emperors. Along the side aisles and in the transepts there are splendid chapels, such as that of Our Lady of the Vow in the side transept and that of John the Baptist on the left side. In the elevated presbytery there is the main altar made by Baldassarre Peruzzi (1532). It is surmounted by a big bronze ciborium made by Vecchietta, put here in 1506 in the place of Duccio's « Maestà ». The marble floor, with its « graffito » and « tarsia » decorations, is one the masterpieces kept in this Cathedral. It consists of 56 tables representing biblical stories, sybils, virtues and various stories, made in different periods of time and by using different technics, from the second half of the 14th century to the middle of the 16th century. Out the more than 40 artists who took part in this work, we mention Matteo di Giovanni, who made « The Slaughter of the Innocents ». On a side, the Sybil Samia, by the same artist.

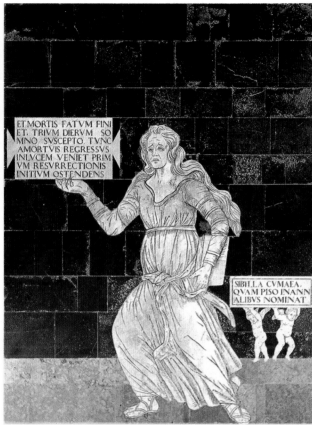

erall view of the marble pavement - View of the ansepts

bano da Cortona - The Cumaean Sibyl

HE CHAPEL OF THE MADONNA EL VOTO

tuated in the Cathedral's right transept, the Chapel as designed by Gian Lorenzo Bernini and built for pe Alexander VII (Fabio Chigi of Siena, 1655-61) in 61. Eliptical in plan, it has a gilded tambour and me divided into eight sections by columns below, lasters in the tambour and ribs in the dome. The apel is richly decorated in the baroque style with arbles, bronzes and other embellishments, includ- g the votive painting on the altar from which it kes its name: the "Madonna del Voto", a painting of e school of Guido da Siena dating to the 13th cen- ry. The Tabernacle on the altar and the Angels in t bronze encircling the icon of the Madonna are the ork of Bernini. The first two statues in the niches to e side of the entrance, St. Jerome and St. Mary agdalen, were also sculpted by Bernini, while those the side of the altar, St. Catherine of Siena and St. ernardine, are by Ercole Ferrata and Antonio Rag- o, both of them pupils of Bernini. The marble pan- s between the columns are decorated with magnif- ent bas-reliefs of scenes from the Life of Mary, ulpted in Rome in 1748. Facing the altar, to the left, a bronze votive statue of "Gratitude" by Arturo Vig- rdi (1918).

Pulpit of Nicola Pisano

Near the hexagon of the dome there is the greatest masterpiece kept in the Cathedral, namely the Pulpit of Nicola di Maestro Pietro (1220-1284), called Nicola Pisano, since he stayed in that Tuscan town for a long time. Nicola is probably of Pugliese origin. He came in contact with the classical circles of the sculptores and architects of the time of Frederick II. Pisano, however, did not simply imitate the classics, but spontaneously assimilated the best aesthetic elements of the classical world. At the same time, he uses classical lines to express new and different ideas and values. And so, his art breaks with past tradition and begins a new one. The pulpit of Siena, one of the best works of the Italian sculpture, is an exceptional expression of this revival and artistic and human greatness of Pisano. It is made of white marble, octagonal, rests on nine columns, of which four have their bases with figures of lions and lionesses killing animals, four are without figures, and the middle one surrounded, below, by eight figures of the Arts. The parapet is adorned with seven reliefs representing stories of Christ from His birth to crucifixion and last judgement, and separated by statues of prophets and angels. In the pendentives of the trilobate arches there are other prophets and in the connections statues of virtues. This pulpit, sculptured between 1265 and 1268, was made a few years before the other one, also famous, of the Cathedral of Pisa, though it is stylistically more advanced than the latter. Instead of the aristocratic and detached figures of the pulpit of Pisa, its simple perspective and narrative solemnity, we have here a greater power of expression, a more free and complex plasticity, a more lively and dramatic partecipation of the characters in their deeds.

In the side photo we see a panel representing « The Nativity » and on the following plate, that of the ➤ « Last Judgement of the Good ».

Detail of the central column of the Pulpit

In the photos above, we see the details of the base of the main column of the pulpit, surrounded by eight figures representing the Seven Liberal Arts and Music; below, the details of the « Flight into Egypt » and the « Crucifixion ». On the right plate, the wonderful panel of the « Crucifixion », a very realistic and dramatic scene. For the first time in the history of sculpture, Christ is a presented by Nicola Pisano as magnificently human, since the sacred history is where human and divine spheres meet.

Crucifixion

High Altar, bronze Angel and St. John the Baptist

The main altar (see photo above) is adorned with the big bronze ciborium made by Vecchietta, and four angels bearing chandeliers, of which two made by Giovanni di Stefano (1489) and two, together with the half figures of angels, are masterpieces of Francesco di Giorgio Martini (1497-99). On the pillars, on bronze corbels, there are eight angels made by Domenico Beccafumi (1548-1550), of which one can be seen in the photo above, on the right side. On a side we can admire a detail of the bronze statue of John the Baptist, by Donatello, placed in the chapel of St. John the Baptist. It was made in Florence and sent to Siena in the October of 1457. It expresses a tormented spirituality and a deep asceticism. This statue date back to the last active years of the Master and was made a little the Repentant Magdalen of the Baptistery of Florence, which it resembles in its style and spirituality.

The Choir

In the apse there is the magnificent wooden choir, which occupies the lower part of the niche for the whole lenght of the three aisles. It was begun in 1363 and finished in 1397. Originally it consisted of more than 90 stalls in a double line, surmounted by canopies and adorned by tabernacles and statues of saints. The part on the sides of the niche is all that remains of the wonderful 14th century work with carvings made by Francesco and Jacopo del Tonghio. The splendid marbles on the back of the stalls were made by Fra' Giovanni of Verona. They were made for the choir of St. Benedict's Convent at Porta Tufi and later placed in the choir of the Cathedral in 1503. They reproduce beautiful still lives and sights of towns. The magnificent middle stalls, in the Renaissance style, were carved by Teseo Bartolini of Pienza and Benedetto di Giovanni of Montepulciano, on design of Riccio, in the second half of the 16th century. The choir, on the whole, is a very refined and magnificent work.

Bell-Tower and Dome of the Cathedral

Dome of the Cathedral: interior

THE DOME – The hexagonal shaped dome was built between 1259 and 1264.
It is supported by six pillars. In each of its corners there are big golden statues of saints, by Ventura Tiparilli and Bastiano di Francesco, resting on columns. Above, some shell-shaped niches change the hexagon into a dodecagon, in which there is a gallery divided by 42 small columns with figures of patriarchs and prophets. The figures were painted in 1481 by Guidoccio Cozzarelli, Benvenuto di Giovanni and Pellegrino di Mariano. Above the gallery there are the asymmetrical cap of the dome and the lantern restored in 1891. This hexagonal dome is very suggestive thanks to its perspective effects. Below it, the floor keeps, within hexagons and rhombs, many biblical stories attributed to Domenico Beccafumi (1486-1551), the most famous Sienese painter in the 16th century. The stories were remade by Alessandro Franchi.
On the outside, the dome is covered by robust ribs and rests on a drum formed by two orders of galleries. The lower one is enclosed by ogive arches supported by double columns, and the upper one has round arches. When in 1376 the building of the New Cathedral stopped and Giovanni Cecco began to complete the facade, they wanted to make it higher and more imposing. So the building had to be raised and the lower order of the small porticoes of the dome was completely smothered.

Piccolomini Altar

PICCOLOMINI ALTAR – The majestic altar, which is along the left aisle, wa made by order of Cardinal Francesco Piccolomini in 1481. It is one of Andre Bregno's works. The Madonna, in the niche above: it attributed to Jacopo dell Quercia, while the delicate Madonna with the Child, placed in the marble altar piece is attributed to Paolo di Giovanni Fei (1381). The statues, made by Miche langelo and placed in the niches, are very interesting: Sts. Paul and Peter langelo and placed in the niches, are very interesting: Sts. Paul and Pete Piccolomini had ordered fifteen of them, but the great artist made only four between 1501 and 1504. These are among the less known works of Michelangelo though they are of a very high artistic value.

Piccolomini Library

In the first span of the left aisle there is the Piccolomini Library. Its building began in 1492 by order of Cardinal Francesco Piccolomini Todeschini, the future Pope Pius III, to collect here the books of the library of Pope Pius II, his uncle on his mother's side. The marble front has elegant decorations by Marrina and is surmounted by a fresco by Bernardino di Betto, named the Pinturicchio (1454-1513), with the Coronation of Pius III.

In the interior of the library, formed by only one rectangular hall, one is struck by its vivid and beautiful colours. In the centre of the hall, on a Renaissance base, there is the group of the «Three Graces» a copy of a Hellenistic original dating back to the III century. This work was donated by Cardinal Piccolomini to be placed in the library. Along the walls, enclosed in pendentives and strips, there are the frescoes made by Pinturicchio between 1505 and 1508. They tell episodes of the life of Enea Silvio Piccolomini, born in Corsignano (Pienza) in 1405, archbishop of Siena, then pope from 1458 to 1464, a famous humanist, diplomat and pontif. This work, however, does not show the freshness and high spirituality of the frescoes in the Baglioni Chapel of Spello or the Borgia's Rooms in the Vatican. Yet these stories strike us with their vivid colours, simple and lively narration, without dramatic emphasis, the illustrative capacities of Pinturicchio, a magnificent decorator.

Piccolomini Library

PICCOLOMINI LIBRARY – Miniated choir-books. In the interior of the library, on benches carved by Antonio Barili in 1496, there are the wonderful choir-books miniated by Liberale of Verona (1445ca-1529) and Girolamo of Cremona (first half of the 15th century). It is a very refined work, which the best example of the miniature art in 15th century Italy. During the previous centuries miniature had much developed mainly in North Italy, where it had put aside the Byzantine models and followed the great Franch-Gothic tradition. In the 13th century the miniature production in Bologna and Emilia was remarkable for quality and quantity. These artists were specialized in illustrating civil and canon law books used in the University. And it was the Bolognese School that influenced the production in central Italy, where it was less rich and interesting, though there were works of great value and originality. Two centuries later, the great masters of the North are still the leaders in the miniature art. And it was in Siena, where they stayed in the second half of the 15th century that Liberale and Girolamo miniated their masterpierces, namely a series of choir-books for the sacristy of the Cathedral. Today they are kept in the Piccolomini library. Together with the choir-books made by these two masters, educated in the Paduan atmosphere of Mantegna's times, whose stay in the Tuscan town influenced the Sienese painting at the end of the 15th century, there are others made by Sienese artists, such as Sano di Pietro, Pellegrino di Mariano and Guidoccio Cozzarelli.

Four of the 10 scenes of the Life of Pius II: from left above: Enea Silvio Piccolomini receives the cardinal's hat from Pope Callisto III; Enea Silvio Piccolomini made Pope with the name of Pius II; Pius II canonizes St. Catherine of Siena; Pius II in Mantova to promote the crusade against the Turks.

Cathedral Museum (Museo dell'Opera del Duomo)

The Museum of the Cathedral is situated in the first three arcades of the right aisle of the New Cathedral. It was constituted in 1870 and later renewed many times. It includes mainly works of art created to embellish the Cathedral and later transferred into the Museum to preserve them or because they were removed from their places and replaced with other works during the restorations in the 16th and 17th centuries. The collection includes sculptural and pictorial groups, bronzes, wooden and terra-cotta objects, gold ware, embroideries and miniature, all works of great artistic value, thanks to which this is one of the richest and most important museums in Italy. In it one finds some famous masterpieces of the Sienese and Tuscan art from the 13th to the 14th century, made by Simon Martini, Pietro Lorenzetti and Jacopo della Quercia, apart from the statues made by Giovanni Pisano for the facade of the Cathedral and the « Maestà » by Duccio di Buoninsegna, all works of incomparable beauty, which are the pride of Siena and some of the greatest artistic expressions in the whole world. On the ground floor, in a hall divided into two sections by a large wrought iron railing dating back to the 14th century, there are, among many other works, fragments of architectonic elements and sculptures of the facade and the interior of the Cathedral; marble plutei of Pisano's school; a front of a Roman sarcophagus dating back to the imperial age; a splendid high-relief dating back to the late maturity of Jacopo della Quercia. Along the walls there are the ten statues sculptured by Giovanni Pisano and removed from the facade of the Cathedral since the second half of the last century. On the first floor there is Duccio's Hall, so called because there is the magnifcent and famous « Maestà ». Here we can admire also the « Nativity of the Virgin » by Pietro Lorenzetti and the « Madonna of Crevole », a work of the young Duccio, coming from St. Cecily's church at Crevole. On the second floor, there is the Treasure Hall, where are kept the most precious sacred furniture of the Cathedral, among which a reliquary of the head of St. Galgano (13th century), a small wooden crucifix of Giovanni Pisano and the wooden busts of the saints Crescentius, Savinus and Victor, made by Francesco di Vandambrino (1409). On the last floor, there is a picture-gallery and the so called « Saloncino dei Conversari », with works of Ambrogio Lorenzetti, Matteo di Giovanni, Sodoma, Domenico Beccafumi. Through a small door of this hall, a few steps lead to the top of the « Facciatone », from where one can enjoy a wonderful view

Cathedral Museum - Lower Hall

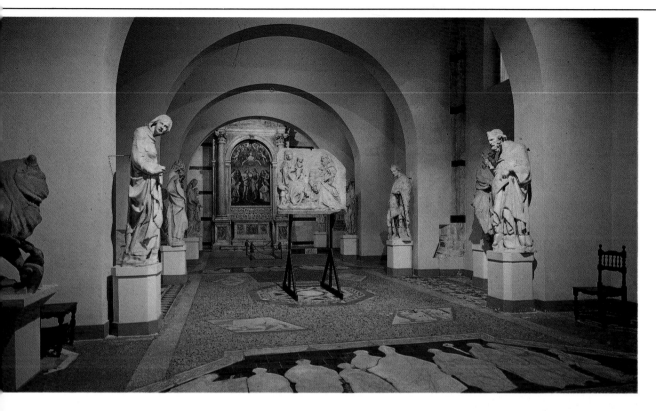

This is the larger lower Hall of the Museum, where are kept the Winged Bull and Lion by Giovanni Pisano, apart from some original fragments of the floor of the Cathedral. At the entrance, after the railing, there is the She-wolf with the Twins, also a work of Pisano and emblem of Siena, and the original work, of which that on the column near the Cathedral is a copy.

In the centre of the hall, on the ground floor, there is, as we have said, the high-relief made by Jacopo della Quercia, representing « The Madonna with the Child, St. Anthony the Abbot and Cardinal Antonio Casini kneeling ». This work, once lost and recently found, dates back to the last period of Jacopo's activity. It is plastically powerful and deeply moral and this fact shows how the artist, in his sculptures, at times resembles Donatello. If, on one side, the rich drapery and a subtle psychologism still connect Jacopo della Quercia with the traditional culture, on the other, the presence of drama, seen as history of which man is the protagonist, is a sign of his partecipation and a consciously humanistic atmosphere.

Giovanni Pisano: Miriam and Abacuc.

MARY OF MOSES – It is perhaps the most beautiful of the ten statues made for the facade of the Cathedral by Giovanni Pisano, born between 1240 and 1245 and educated under shelter of his father's art. However, he went for his own way, rejecting the Hellenic serenity of Nicola and preferring the transalpine Gothic sculpture to it.

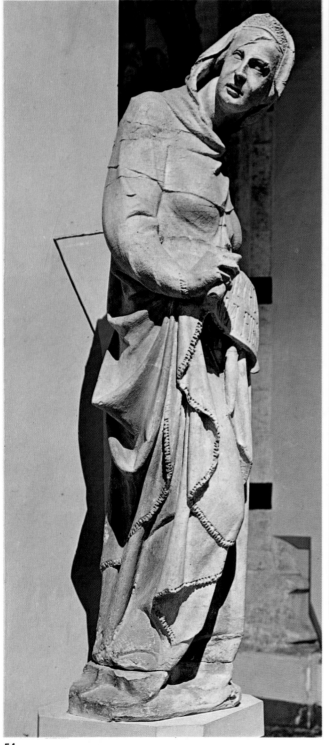

ABACUC – These statues, among which the pathetic Abacuc, were made between 1285 and 1296. They represent biblical figures, ancient philosophers and prophets, taller than usual. They constitute one of the most important and daring work of the Gothic and European sculptural art and a masterpiece of Giovanni Pisano.

Giovanni Pisano: Moses, Sibyl and Isaiah

MOSES, SIBYL, ISAIAH — These graceful figures, with that spiral drapery and the brusque movement with their heads, show an extraordinary vitality, which overcomes matter and expresses itself mainly in the faces with their well-defined features. Here we find the whole world of Pisano — a dramatic and, at times, tormented world, where he combines plastic forms with feelings on a plane we could call expressionistic. Placing himself between the classicism of his father's art and the Gothic of the transalpine and specially French art, he reaches the height of his poetical research, trying to create an impetuous and dramatic vision.

The Maestà (Duccio di Buoninsegna)

The magnificent « Maestà » is praised by the chroniclers of that time, who describe the parade by which this work was taken into the church by the people and local authorities. It is the masterpiece of Duccio di Buoninsegna (1278-1318), the first great Sienese artist, who knew how to change various elements into poetical themes by combining the aulic preciosity of the Byzantine patterns with the human lyricism of the French Gothic style. With the « Maestà » the 13th century pictorical experience comes to an end and a new age begins. The great development of the 14th century Sienese school is mainly due to him. The monumental painting, ordered on October 9, 1308 and completed after about three years, had to adorn the main alter of the Cathedral, where it was placed on June 9, 1311, but it was removed two centuries later. Then it was dismembered and transferred in 1876 into the Museum of the Cathedral. On its front there is the Madonna with the Child among worshiping angels and saints. On the back, in front of the « Maestà », divided into 26 parts, are represented episodes of the Passion of Christ, separated by a large middle strip which marks a break between the first scenes, in the lower order, and the last ones, in the upper order. Once this work had a predella with Stories of Christ's Childhood (seven on the front) and His Public life (ten on the back), and a Gothic gable including 16 panels with episodes of the Life of the Madonna(on the front) and the Risen Christ (on the back). Out of these latter parts, five panels got lost, while some others are now kept in museums and foreign collections; others, 19 panels, are kept in the Museum together with the front and the back of the work.

Episodes of the Passion of Christ

Here we can admire the 26 panels of the back, representing the Stories of the Passions of Christ, from the Entry in Jerusalem to the Apparitions at Emmaus, where a new and different harmony is created by the play of colours and lines, in a constant and various rythm, including each scene and the scenes of the whole cycle. In the middle, the panel of the Crucifixion, larger than the others, and tragically beautiful. On a golden background, above a crowd of various people, the Christ divides the scene in a dramatic crescendo, where Duccio's art reaches the height of poetry.

The 26 panels – From above and from left to right:
1/2 - Christ sent to Pilate and Christ before Herod. 3/4 - The Scourging and Crowning with Thorns. 5/6 - Going up to Calvary and Pilate washing his hand. 7 - The Crucifixion. 8/9 - Christ taken down from the cross and buried. 10/11 - Mary at the Tomb and the Descent into the Limbus. 12/13 - Apparition at Emmaus and « Noli me tangere » (Do not touch me).

Lower panels
14 - Jesus entering Jerusalem. 15/16 - Jesus washing His disciples' feet and the Last Supper. 17/18 - Judas' Pact and Christ's Farewell. 19/20 - Judas' kiss and Prayer in the Garden. 21/22 - Christ before Annah and Peter's Denial. 23/24 - Christ beaten and Christ before

Crucifixion

Picture Gallery (Pinacoteca)

In the first hall of the picture-gallery situated on the third floor of the Museum, among some interesting works of the Sienese school, there is the so called "Madonna with large eyes", dating back to the beginning of the 13th century. It is one of the oldest works of the Sienese painting art. Once it was on the main altar of the Cathedral, before the Maestà was placed there. The people of Siena knelt before it, before the battle of Montaperti, which took place in 1260.

In the other two photos are represented the panels of the Coronation of the "Maestà", with the Death of Mary and the Funeral of Mary. Duccio was able to express the deep and poetical meanings of each episode.

Birth of Mary (Pietro Lorenzetti)

THE NATIVITY OF MARY – Pietro Lorenzetti – (Detail). It is situated in the Hall of the Maestà. It is the last known work of Lorenzetti (1280 ca - 1348), who, among the early 13th century masters, follows Giotto more closely. Here the artist, putting aside the traditional division of the polyptics, has represented only one scene in the right panel and in the middle one, with a new perspective and greater narrative vivacity.

The Baptistery

The Baptistery, called also « Pieve di San Giovanni », rises on the back of the Cathedral and is the base of the continuation of its head, like a crypt. Its facade, begun in 1317 and again in 1382, erroneously attributed to Giacomo di Mino del Pellicciaio, was probably made by Domenico d'Agostino. It shows a true decorative preciosity. Incomplete in its upper part, it is mostly made of white marble and consists of three large portals flanked with small columns and marble decorations. In the middle there are pensile arches and, above, blind ogive windows. On the floor, before the portals, there are marble graffitoes representing the Sacraments of Baptism and Confirmation; that before the left door, representing the « Birth of Man » with a woman in labour and a new-born baby, is one of the works of Bartolomeo di Mariano, called « Mandriano » (1450). The other two, with the scene of the Baptism before the main door and Confirmation before the right portal, were made by Antonio Federighi (1451). The interior of the Baptistery is vast and luminous. It was completed in 1325 under the direction of Camaino di Crescentino. It is rectangular and divided into three aisles. Its vaults, apse and two lunettes above the side altars are completely covered with frescoes. Those made by Lorenzo di Pietro, called Vecchietta (1447-1450) are very precious. They occupy the vaults where are represented the Articles of the Creed, the Prophets and the Sybils, and the walls of the apse with two scenes of the life of Christ, the « Scourging » and « Going to Calvary ». The other paintings were made by Michele di Matteo of Bologna and Benvenuto di Giovanni (late 15th century).

Baptismal Font: Capture of John the Baptist (Lorenzo Ghiber

THE FONT, erected on two steps in the centre of the church, has, at its base, a hexagonal basin and, above, a pillar supporting a hexagonal ciborium. The ciborium, designed by Jacopo della Quercia, is surmonted by a small column on which rests a beautiful statue of the Baptist, made by Jacopo. The small well, made from 1417 on by Sano di Matteo, Nanni di Jacopo of Lucca and Jacopo di Corso of Florence, on design erroneously attributed to Jacopo della Quercia, has six lcw-reliefs in golden bronze, which extol the life of St. John the Baptist. On the plate we see one of the low-reliefe made by Lorenzetti Ghiberti (1378-1455), who made also the famous « Gates of Heaven » of the Florence Baptistery. Here is represented the « Arrest of the a Baptist », a very refined work, very elegant in its forms and serene plasticity.

The Baptismal Font with Ciborium (Jacopo della Quercia)

Here we can at last admire the magnificent Font. The reliefs around the small well begin, on the side towards the altar, with « The Angel announcing Baptist's Birth to Zechariah », by Jacopo della Quercia (1428-29) and go on with the « Baptist's Birth » and the « Baptist's Preaching » by Giovanni di Turino (1427), the « Baptism of Christ » and the « Arrest of the Baptist » by Lorenzo Ghiberti (1427) and « Herod's Banquet » by Donatello (1427). With the six low-reliefs alternate some statues made by Donatello « Faith » and « Hope », by Giovanni di Turino, « Justice » « Charity » and « Providence » and by Goro di Ser Neroccio « Fortitude ». The statues of prophets adorning the ciborium in the niches, were made by Jacopo della Quercia, while Turino made the delicate Madonna with the Child on the door. Donatello and Giovanni di Turino made also the bronze angels on the front of the tabernacle. Many artists took part in the building of the Font. In spite of this, it is stylistically uniform and can be considered a true masterpiece of the plastic and scultural art.

BAPTISMAL FONT
« The Baptism of Jesus »
by Lorenzo Ghiberti;
« The Angel announces
to Zechariah the Baptist's Birth », by Jacopo
della Quercia, and « Herod's Banquet » by Donatello.

The Pinacoteca Nazionale (Picture Gallery)

The National Picture-Gallery of Siena is situated in Palazzo Buonsignori, one of the most elegant late-Gothic buildings of the town. It includes a collection of works which are very important for the knowledge of the sienese painting art from the end of the 12th century to the first half of the 17th century. Its origin dates back to the 18th century, when the abbot Giuseppe Ciaccheri collected some paintings to donate them to the town of Siena. Later on, works coming from various donations, store-rooms, churches, convents, religious and lay associations, which had been suppressed, enriched the collection. It was housed, first, in the Institute of Fine Arts, later, in 1930, in Palazzo Buonsignori, under the State Administration, The Picture Gallery keeps about 700 paintings arranged in 28 halls according tho chronological order or various styles. The greatest masters and less known painters are present here with some of their works. Works which are masterpieces known all over the world, are exhibited together with less important works. All of them, however, contribute to form an incomparably valuable patrimony and the most peculiar testimony of the painting school of Siena, which was, as Roberto Paribeni said, « the perfect image of a world, happy and gentle synthesis of the great spiritual riches of Italy ». Below, is represented the facade of Palazzo Buonsignori, built after 1440 by Giovanni di Guccio Bichi, a very rich Sienese banker, and a few years later sold to Tegliacci brothers. In 1476 it was bought by the Buonsignori family, whose last descendant donated it to the town to be used as a museum. The brick facade, with a stone base is one of the last examples of Gothic architecture. Below it has some blind arches, and on the first and second floors there are elegant three-mullioned windows divided by a cornice of pensile arches. Among the merlons of the crowning there are marble panels with stucco heads.

MADONNA OF THE FRANCISCANS – It dates back around 1300. It is one of the most renowned works ➤ of Duccio di Boninsegna. His art, though grounded in the ancient Byzantine tradition, shows a very refined and pathetically human emphasis.

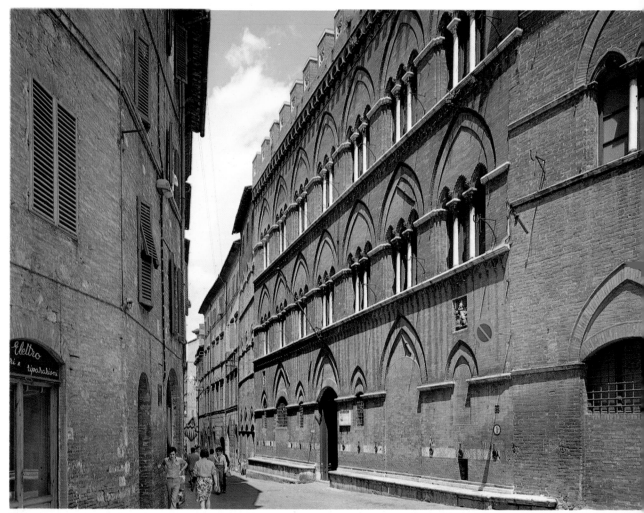

The Madonna of the Franciscans (Duccio di Buoninsegna)

THE ADORATION OF T|
MAGI – It is probably t|
masterpiece of Bartolo di F|
di and was made betwe|
1370 and 1380. It is a v|
fine work, thanks to its ri|
details, vivid colours; t|
ANNUNCIATION, a very fi|
and lyric work of Frances|
di Giorgio Martini, one of |
most complex and charm|
artistic personalities in t|
late 15th century. On a si|
POLYPTYC OF ST. DOROTH|
by Ambrogio Lorenzetti. T|
work, made around 1332, |
presents the Madonna w|
the Child, St. Mary Magda|
in the left panel and St. D|
rothy in the right one.

The small «MAESTA'», on the right side, is another very fine work of Ambrogio Lorenzetti who made it around 1340. It is very important because of its perspecitve anticipations and great solemnity.

CHRIST AT THE PILLAR, by Giovanni Antonio Bazzi, called SODOMA (1477-1549). It is a spiritually and stilistically refined work, which was a part of a greater work made between 1511 and 1514 for the convent of St. Francis in Siena.

THE ADORATION OF THE SHEPHERDS, by Taddeo di Bartolo (1362-1422), dating back to the end of the 14th century, a very sober and genuine work.

The Pinacoteca Nazionale (Picture Gallery)

A TOWN ON THE SEA, by Ambrogio Lorenzetti. This small painting and the other one on the side page, come from the Archives of the Municipality and probably represent places of the ancient State of Siena. This town on the sea is probably Talamone, a port of the Republic. Thanks to its delicate colours and clear forms, the two paintings constitute some of the finest works kept in the Picture-Gallery. In them reality is transformed into a magically charming atmosphere. They are very interesting not only because of their artistic value, but also because they are the first paintings of the European art, which represent landscapes.

THE FLIGHT TO EGYPT — Together with two other paintings, THE PRESENTATION OF MARY IN THE TEMPLE and THE CRUCIFIXION, this work is a part of a predella, made in 1436 by Giovanni di Paolo (1399-1482). This artist's poetry goes beyond reality and gets into a trascendent sphere.

The Pinacoteca Nazionale (Picture Gallery)

CASTLE ON THE BANKS OF A LAKE, by Ambrogio Lorenzetti is not a disciple of Pietro, his elder brother, but follows, Cimabue, Giotto and Simone Martini. He follows these great artists through the minor personalities who constitute the environment of that time. In the case of this fine painting, the artist was probably inspired by a garrison of the Sienese Republic, situated on the lake of Chiusi or on the Trasimeno.
While we see towers and embattled walls all crowded in the centre of the preceding painting, here we have a country landscape, which in an atmosphere of quiet and solitude, shows a deep and charming lyricism.

THE ROLY FAMILY WITH ST. JOHN AS A CHILD, by Pinturicchio. It dates back to the late years of this artist, who stayed in Siena for a long time to fresco the vaults of the Piccolomini Library. This work, coming from the Convent of Campansi, shows all the characteristics of the Umbrian painter, who was an elegant and magnificent decorator.

The Pinacoteca Nazionale (Picture Gallery)

THE MADONNA APPEARS TO CAL-
LISTUS IIII (1456), by Sano di Pietro (1406-1481). Apart from this
painting, this artist's production is
largely present in other three halls
of the Picture-Gallery.

ST. JEROME IN THE DESERT — It
belongs to a triptych made in 1436,
whose upper part is now in the
Basilica of the Observance near
Siena. For a long time it was attributed to Sassetta. Today it is
thought to be the work of an artist
who painted in a style similar to
that of Salsetta and called the
« Master of the Observance ».

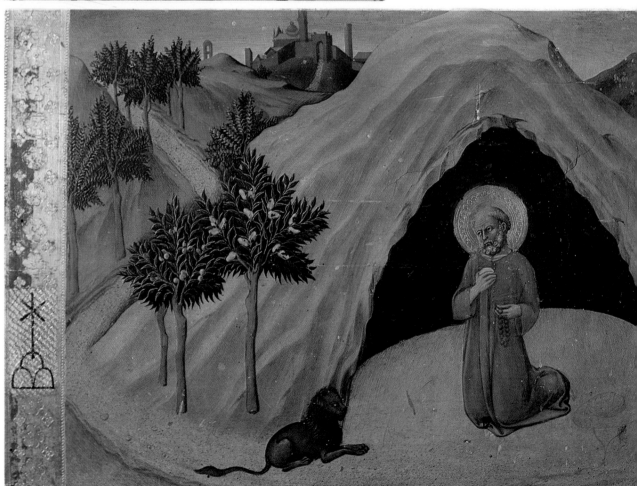

The Pinacoteca Nazionale (Picture Gallery)

THE ANNUNCIATION, by Ambrogio Lorenzetti. This work is signed and dated 1344. It is the last known work of the great painter. In it we note the particularly well chosen colours, its rich decorations, a new perspective, together with a conscious serenity by which the Mistery is interpreted.

PORTRAIT OF ELISABETH QUEEN OF ENGLAND, attributed to Federico Zuccari (1542-1606). In the same hall there are works of G.B. Moroni, Scarsellino, Bernardo Strozzi and Padovanino, all painters of the 17th and 18th centuries.

THE NATIVITY, by Andrea di Bartolo (1389-1428), a Sienese painter, son of Bartolo di Fredi, whose disciple and co-operator he was. His style, though influenced by his father's, shows a greater freedom as regards composition and chromatic vividness.

MADONNA ON A THRONE, a detail of the Ancona of Carmel, painted by Pietro Lorenzetti in 1328-1329 for the Church of Carmel in Siena. The great ancona dismembered in 1500, included a central panel with the Madonna on a throne, with St. Nicholas of Bari and the Prophet Elijah on her sides, and a predella with five panels, in which are represented the foundation and the first events of the Carmelite Order. The great statuesque plasticity, the severe harmony of the few dominating colours and a dynamic tension of its lines, make of this work one of the masterpieces of the artist's mautrity.

The Pinacoteca Nazionale (Picture Gallery)

THE LAST SUPPER, by Stefano di Giovanni called Sassetta (about 1392-1450). This painting was a part of an ancona made between 1423 and 1426 for the Chapel of the Wool-workers' Guild of Siena. It is the first work of Sassetta, and very important for the history of the Sienese painting art in the 15th century. In it we perceive the influence of Simone Martini and Pietro Lorenzetti, but their styles are re-interpreted in a new and modern manner. Its colour is intensely luminous and transparent.

Λ
MADONNA WITH THE CHILD (a detail), by Matteo di Giovanni (1430-1495), a remarkable work for its pure and simple lines.

LUCRECE, of the school of Luke Cranach (1472-1553), a German painter who made many portraits and kept an active workshop at the service of various princely courst of Germany. In the same hall there are works of other Fleminsh and German masters.

The Last Supper (Sassetta - Stefano di Giovanni)

The Pinacoteca Nazionale (Picture Gallery)

THE MYSTICAL MARRIAGE OF ST. CATHERINE OF ALEXANDRIA, by Michelino of Besozzo (of whom we have informations from 1388 to 1442).
This painter was very important as far as the international painting art in Lombardia is concerned.
The painting here exhibited is a particular example of his over-refined decorative art.

OUR LADY OF SORROWS, by Ugolino di Nerio, a Sienese painter of the first half of the XVth century.
In his art, he follows Duccio and the Lorenzetti's circle.

The Pinacoteca Nazionale (Picture Gallery)

MADONNA AND CHILD WITH ST. JOHN THE BAP
TIST AND ST. ANDREW by Neroccio di Bartolomeo
Landi (1447-1500). A painter and sculptor, he was a
pupil of Vecchietta, and his works mark the epilogu
of the Sienese figurative tradition. More so than in
his sculptures, he expressed in his paintings a deli
cate linear style.

THE NATIVITY OF JESUS by Pietro di Domenico
(1457-1503). Delicate in inspiration and beautiful in it
detail, this is the only signed work by the artist who
was very active in the Marche, following in the foo
steps of Gentile da Fabriano and the Umbrian pain
ers, especially Pinturicchio.

GUIDO DA SIENA (?), a painter of the mid-13th centu
ry: *Madonna and Child with Two Angels*.
Apart from this painting, other works have been attri
buted to Guido, including a fine altar-frontal also dis
played in the Pinacoteca Nazionale.

The Pinacoteca Nazionale (Picture Gallery)

POPE HONORIUS APPROV-ING THE RULE OF THE CAR-MELITES - One of the predel-a panels of Pietro Lorenzet-i's great altarpiece. In these little painted episodes the artist achieved a kind of mag-cal beauty, and succeeds in raising even the most humble aspects of daily life to the level of poetry.

TADDEO DI BARTOLO (1362-1422), *The Adoration of the Magi.*
In the present painting, simi-ar to that of the Adoration of the Shepherds, the artist seems deliberately to empha-size the richness of the de-ails and the vividness of the colours.

The city of Siena by night

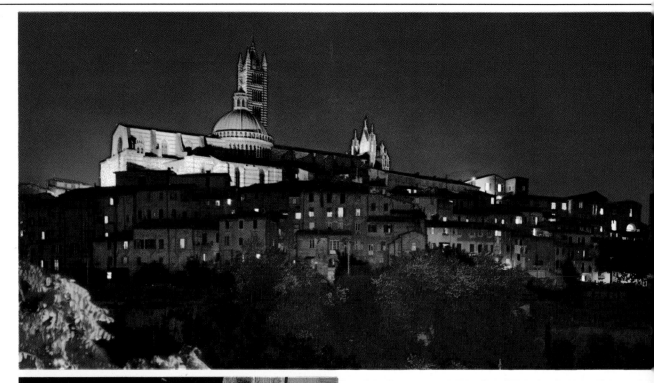

By night Siena is immersed in a peculiar and charming atmosphere, which the tourist perceive when admiring the noble elegance of the Palazzo Pubblico and the solemn magnificence of the Cathedral, or walking along the old and picturesque alleys climbing up among houses leaning one against the other among vaults and buttresses. It is a town with a magic scenography, which seems to have come out of a fairy-story book.

The city of Siena seen by night and at sunset

Dawn and dusk are two magical moments in Siena's day. The profiles of the city's most important monuments seem to be animated with life when the last rays of the sun illuminate them with touches of saffron and gold. Similarly the level and unreal light of dawn creates a thousand hues of pink, purple and fiery red on the undulating Sienese countryside, highlighting an unusual aspect of the fantastic panorama. By contrast, the artificial light that illuminates the Piazza del Campo and the Palazzo Pubblico seems almost to arouse a sense of mystery, broken only by the rhythmic pealing of the bells that punctuate with their sound the passage of the night.

Views of the city of Siena

ST. JOSEPH'S ARCH AND FOUNTAIN of the Contrada of the Wave. Each contrada has a small fountain placed along the main street or near the Oratory and bearing a small statue representing the emblem of the contrada. On the feast of the Patron Saint the children born during the year are baptized with the water springing from these fountains.

CHURCH OF HOLY MARY OF THE SERVANTS — This church was built in the 13th century and later enlarged. It rises on the top of a high flight of steps, on a solitary square with trees. The simple and austere facade has only one portal surmounted by two rose-windows, while the Romanesque belfry with one-mullioned windows which in the upper part become four-mullioned windows. The interior, with Renaissance aisles and Gothic transept and apse, keeps precious works of art.

Oratory of St. Bernardine

St. Bernardine's Oratory is on the right side of St. Francis' Square, where the basilica of St. Francis rises. This church was built in 1326 on the place of a pre-existing small church and later many times modified. Its interior is very interesting for its architectonic structure and frescoes. The nearby old Convent of St. Francis, recently restored, houses the Faculty of Economical and Banking Sciences of the University.

The Oratory consists of two superimposed orders, the lower oratory and the upper oratory. It was built in the 15th century on the place where St. Bernardine used to pray. Bernardine was born in Massa Marittima in 1380 and died in L'Aquila in 1444. He devoted himself to humanistic and law studies, till he joined the Franciscan Order, when he was 22. He began his preaching ministery in Genova, and travelled all over Northern and Central Italy. He distinguished himself for his genuineness. Bernardine was a providential reformer for the Franciscan Order and for the Catholic world the promoter of a new spiritual zeal, which influenced the religious and civil life of his times.

In the photo we can admire the interesting upper oratory, with ceiling and wooden walls stuccoed by Ventura Turapilli in 1496. Among the pillars there are very precious frescoes made by Sodoma, Girolamo del Pacchia and Domenico Beccafumi. « St. Francis of Assisi » by Sodoma, is perhaps the most beatiful of these frescoes. The lower oratory is decorated by 17th century paintings: a « Madonna with the Child and Sts. Bartholomew and Ansanus » by Andrea del Brescianino is placed near the altar, on whose sides there are two niches with the statues of St. Bernardine and St. Catherine, painted in white, dating back to the 17th century. Near the altar there are some precious works, such as a « Madonna with the Child » in painted wood of the school of Jacopo della Quercia, a « Madonna » by Sano di Pietro and a very delicate low-relief made by Giovanni d'Agostino.

Basilica of San Domenico

The imposing basilica of St. Dominic dominates the hill, at whose foot there is Fonte Branda, the most beautiful and famous of the many Sienese fortified fountains. This work, in a severe Gothic style and all in bricks, was begun in 126 by the Dominicans who built the rectangular nave and the open truss ceiling. Around 1300 they built the crypt which, being so large, is practically a church, so much so that it was called the Lower Church or Church of the Dead, because it housed some tombs. It was restored in 1935. It consists of one large room with three aisles and keeps works of Sodoma, Ventura Salimbeni, Sano di Pietro and Turino di Sano. The belfry was built in 1340 and in the 14th century the building of the basilica went on and was completed in 1465. It was severely damaged by fire in 1532 and earthquake in 1779. Later it was restored and today it has its original structure. The Egyptian cross-shaped interior has only one nave and is very simple and imposing. The chapel of St. Catherine, on the right wall, is very interesting. In it there are frescoes made by Sodoma, and considered to be some of his masterpieces, such as « St. Catherine's Ecstasy and Fainting Fit », and the chapel of the vaults, which keeps, near the altar, a painting of Andrea Vanni, representing St. Catherine of Siena, considered to be the only true portrait of Catherine Benincasa. Together with other important works of art, particularly noteworthy are the ciborium and two marble angels near the main altar of the basilica, made by Benedetto da Maiano around 1475, two beautiful paintings of Matteo di Giovanni (1479) and a fresco by Pietro Lorenzetti. From the right side of the facade one gets into the cloister of St. Dominic, built in 1425, almost completely remade in 1951, where some fragments of frescoes made by Lippo Memmi and Andrea Vanni (14th century) have been found.

BASILICA OF ST. DOMINIC

The elegant square belfry made of bricks, quite modified during the 18th century, and the incomplete facade. On its left side there were the niches in which some aristocratic tombs were placed. Below: the fresco representing st. Catherine portrait made by Andrea Vanni, a disciple of hers, and on the right side: « St. Barbara on a throne among angels and Sts. Magdalen and Catherine »; in the lunette, « Epiphany », a masterpiece of Matteo di Giovanni, made in 1479. The painting is in the second chapel of the left transpet.

On the plate of the next page, a partial view of Siena seen from the church of St. Dominic, dominated by the Tower of Mangia and the imposing building of the Cathedral and its belfry. ➤➤

Panoramic view of Siena from the Basilica of San Domeni

Chapel of Saint Catherine

ST. CATHERINE'S CHAPEL – Near the altar there is a marble tabernacle, made by Giovanni di Stefano in 1466, containing Catherine's head. The chapel was almost completely frescoed by Sodoma, of whom we see on the left side: « The saint interceding for the execution of Niccolò di Tuldo », and on the right: « St. Catherine's fainting fit ». They are very valuable paintings specially for the figure of Catherine and the harmony of the group.

On a side: « The saint delivering a possessed person », an oil-painting on wall, by Francesco Vanni (1593). The pictorial decorations of the pillars and the 16th century marble floor are very interesting.

Basilica of San Domenico: the Crypt

THE CRYPT — In the photo above, on the left, one can see the crypt used as partial foundation of the temple. It is large and luminous and has a cross-vault and ample modern glass windows made by Fiorenzo Joni. On the main altar there is a very precious cross painted by Sano di Pietro. Other interesting works are a painting of Sodoma and assistants, representing « The Eternal Father and 4 saints », a painting representing the Madonna, attributed to Paolo di Giovanni Fei or to Francesco di Vannucci (second half of the 14th century), and a « Crucifixion and Saints » by Ventura Salimbeni.
Below, on the right side: a wooden crucifix recently found in the crypt. The plaster covering it, was removed by a friar. This work of an unknown artist, is very valuable and dates back probably to the 14th century.

The Palazzo Chigi Saracini

CHIGI SARACINI PALACE – It was begun in the 12th century and completed in the first half of the 14th century and many times restored during the following centuries. The Chigi Saracini Palace, once Marescotti Palace, is austere and graceful, magnificent and elegant at the same time. It is slightly bent in its front. It is made of stone and bricks with two orders of three-mullioned windows and a stone docked tower. Since 1932 it is the seat of the Chigian Musical Academy, an important centre for musical specialized studies, which every year, in July, organizes the Sieneses musical week. From the dark passage-way leading to the picturesque courtyard, one gets into the palace, which has very beautiful rooms, precious furniture, and interesting music-halls with a collections of ancient musical instruments. Many works of art, some of them very valuable, are kept in it.

The Palazzo Salimbeni

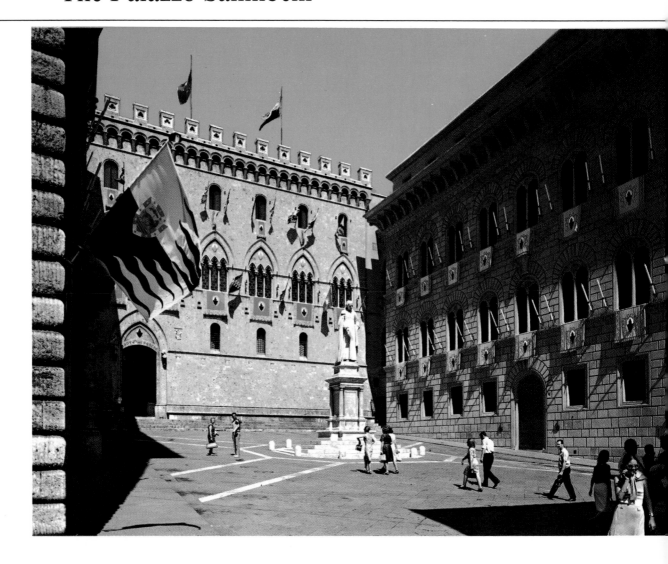

SALIMBENI SQUARE — This square, quiet and not very large, is enclosed on three sides by monumental palaces. On the background there is the front of Salimbeni Palace. It is a 14th century Gothic building, enlarged and restored in 1879 by Giuseppe Partini. It consists of three floors, of which the middle one is adorned with six elegant three-mullioned windows surmounted by ogive arches bearing the coat-of-arms. This palace is the seat of the oldest Italian credit institution, the « Monte dei Paschi di Siena », founded in 1472. On the right side of the square there is the Renaissance Spannocchi Palace, begun by Giuliano da Maiano in 1470 for Ambrogio Spannocchi, treasurer of Pius II, then completed by Partini in 1880. The ashlar facade presents, below, some rectangular windows and, above, two orders of mullioned windows. In front of it there is Tantucci del Riccio Palace, built in 1548.
In the centre of the square there is the monument to the economist Sallustio Bandini, made by Tito Scarocchi in 1882.

TOLOMEI PALACE — It existed already in 1205, but was completely remade after 1267. It is the oldest one of the Sienese private palaces. It is made of stone and presents, on the facade, two orders of rectangular mullioned windows surmounted by ogive arches, in which the tri-lobes are outlined. The Palace houses now the seat of the Saving Bank of Florence. In front of this palace, there is the church of St. Christophere of Romanesque origin, where the Council of the Republic used to meet before the Palazzo Pubblico was built.

The Palazzo Tolomei

The Walls and Gates of Siena

The mark of the communal culture, which has been kept intact through the centuries, characterizes even today this town, not noly in its monuments, but also in the whole area within the old city-walls. Dark and winding alleys among houses arranged according a very picturesque order, small sunny squares and narrow passage-ways, courtyards and archivolts connecting very near walls, streets sloping down till they meet in the centre of the town, in the large square of the « Campo », magnificent churches and houses, incomparable testimonies of culture and creative genius – this is the historical centre of Siena, the heart of a noble and gentle town, where all speaks of history and art.
Siena rises on three hills which, limited by the Arbia and Elsa, meet near the Campo (Field), taking so the shape of an upside-down Y. It is divided in three main districts called Terzi or Terzieri: the district of the Town, that of « San Martino » and that of « Camollia ». These main districts include some other smaler districts – the 17 « Contrade », each having its own flag, seat and church. All around Siena there are the powerful medieval walls about 7 kilometres long and including the many gates we can see in the photos on these pages.

CAMOLLIA GATE, built in the 14th century and re-built in 1604 on designs of Alessandro Casolani. It is situated to the north of the town and bears on the outside front of the arch an inscription welcoming the visitor: COR MAGIS TIBI SEN PANDIT (Siena opens her heart to you more than this gate).

ST. BARBARA FORT OR MEDICEAN FORTRESS - It was built in 1560 by Cosimo I. It occupies a quadrangular area and has robust towers on each corner. From the bastions, changed into public gardens in 1937, one can enjoy a wonderful view of the town and surrounding hills.

OUTER PORT - It consists of a high embattled portal, almost all in stone. It dates back to the 14th century and constituted the advanced fortifications of the town to the north.

THE PORTA ROMANA - This crenellated gateway dates to 1327 and preserves under its arch the only known fresco painting by Sassetta depicting "Glory of Angels playing Musical Instruments". Attributed to Agnolo Ventura (1327), this gate too is fortified by an outer barbican.

THE PORTA OVILE, dating to the 14th century and equipped with an outer barbican. Walled into the latter to the left is a "Madonna and Child", tabernacle and fresco by Sano di Pietro.

THE PORTA PISPINI - This is the ancient city gate of San Viene, to which the tower attributed to Minuccio di Rinaldo was added in 1326. It is decorated by a fresco of "Angels in Glory", the precious remains of a "Navitiy" by Sodoma.

House of Saint Catherine and Sanctuary of St. Catherir

Catherine Benincasa (1347-1480) lived in this house, with its beautiful Renaissance portal in stone and a fine brick loggia. Catherine vigorously expressed the necessity of a deep renewal in the Church. She was canonized by Pius II in 1461 and in 1939 was declared by Pius XII patron saint of Italy. In the 15th century the house of Catherine was transformed into a sanctuary. Below: the Portico of the Italian Free Cities — double outside loggia, a part of St. Catherine's Sanctuary, built in 1941.

FONTE BRANDA - It is the most famous one of the many fountains of Siena, already existing in 1081. It was later enlarged by Bellamino and remade in 1246 by Giovanni di Stefano. Probably it was so called after a nearby house belonging to a certain Brando or Ildebrando, or else after an old Brandi family. It is made of briks and has on its front three large ogive arches, surmounted by gables and adorned with merlons and four leonine gargolyes with the emblem of Siena in the middle. The fountain is dominated by the apse of the basilica of St. Dominic.

The Fonte Branda

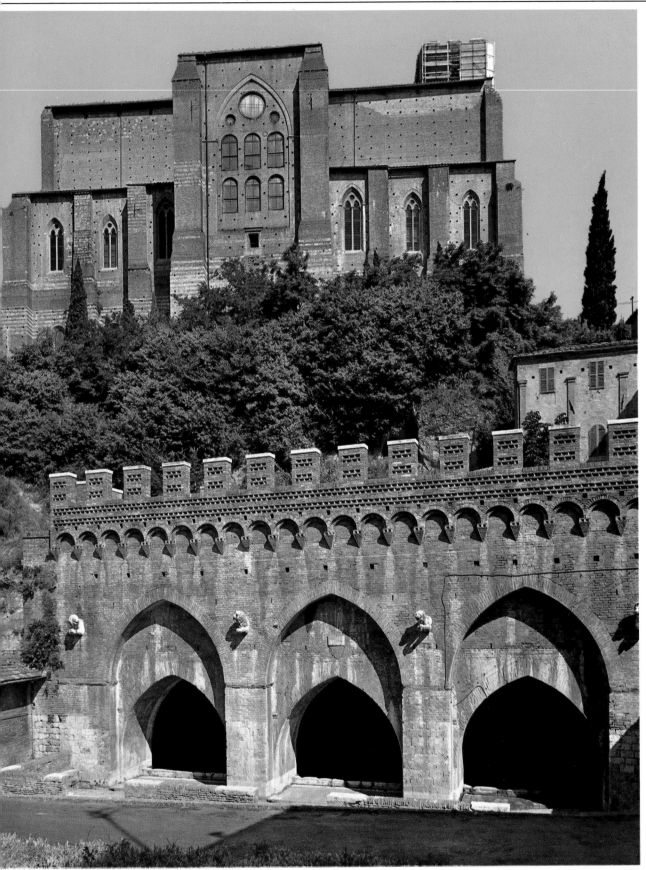

Archivio di Stato and the "Tavolette della Biccherna"

The State Archives are in the important Piccolomini Palace, the most beautiful building of Siena, begun in 1469 by Pietro Paolo Pirrina, probably on designs of Bernardo Rossellino.

The Archives, constituted in 1775 and placed in 1855 in the same palace, includes a large collection of records, which are very important for the knowledge of the Political, civil and artistic life of Siena and the whole province. They include parchments, more than 60.000 since the year 736, various laws of the Republic, letters and acts of the financial and judicial administration. The most interesting part of the collection has been arranged in three halls. It includes records concerning events and people mentioned by Dante in his Comedy; imperial credentials and papal bulls, the will of Giovanni Boccaccio, autographs and letters of famous men and women, artists, and records concerning famous works, such as the « Maestà » of Duccio, The Fonte and the Pulpit of Nicola Pisano. There are also commercial records and records concerning the Sienese studies, the Medici, the siege and fall of the town and the Palio. There is also an interesting collection of miniated statutes, such as the so called « Caleffo dell'Assunta » of Niccolò di Ser Sozzo Tegliacci (1334) and the « Statute of Merchandise », miniated by Sano di Pietro in 1472. Very precious from the historical and artistic points of view are the « Tablets of Biccherna », of which we reproduce here ten specimens, with the permission of the Ministry of Cultural and Environing Goods and of the State Archives of Siena. This collection consists of painted tablets used to cover, every six months, the books of the administrations of « Biccherna » and « Gabella ». The magistrates whorun the main financial offices of the Republic, changed every six monhts. At the end of their term they had their coats-of-arms and a sacred or symbolical scene commemorating the most important event of that period, painted in the wooden cover of the books. These tablets dated from 1268 to 1659, were painted by the most renowned masters of that time, such as Ambrogio and Pietro Lorenzetti, Giovanni di Paolo, Vecchietta, Sano di Pietro, Francesco di Giorgio Martini, Neroccio di Bartolomeo Landi, Domenico Beccafumi; just to mention only some of them. Apart from those of Biccherna, in the Archives there are also other tablets belonging to the books of the Hospital of « Santa Maria della Scala » and various Sienese institutions.

« Mystical Marriage of the Sts. Catherine of Alexandria and Catherine of Siena ».
Domenico Beccafumi – January-December 1548. This work represent the Mystical Marriage, showing the Madonna seating while the Child Jesus puts the rings on the fingers of the two Virgins keeling on his sides. At the lower centre there is the coat of arms of the Camarlingo Marinelli and other coat of arms of noble families.

« The Administration of Justice »

It was made by unknown author who received 30 « soldi » for his work. It refers to January-June of the year 1237. It was made at the time of Taddeo, Count of Urbino, of Montefeltro, mayor of Siena during the first semester of 1273. In the upper part are painted the coats of arms of the four Purveyors in charge. Enea di Rinaldo Piccolomini was Camarlingo « pro tempore ». In the lower part, we see the Mayor condemning a citizen. The administration of Justice was one of the few tasks of the Mayor after the institution in 1252 of the office of Captain of the People.

« The Good Governmnet of Siena »

Ambrogio Lorenzetti – July-June 1344 – The Good Government is represented by an austere and dignified figure. The four letters: C(ivitas) S(enarum) C(ivitas) V(irginis), that means « The Town of Siena is the Town of the Virgin », placed on the sides of the head, show the devotion of Siena to the Virgin to whom all the people offered themselves in order to ask her protection during the battle of Monteaperti. The coats of arms belong to the Forteguerri, Mignanelli and Ranuccini families, to which belonged the three Executors in charge, mentioned in the inscription.

« Don Ghiffolino Nazi, Abbot of San Donato, Camerlingo ».

◄ Coats of arms of four Purveyors – January-June of the year 1263. Unknown author: it is a copy of the original once belonging to the Ramboux collection of Colonia and sold in 1867. The name of the owner of the original is unknown. This composition represents the coats of arms of the four Purveyors in charge, whose names are mentioned in the inscription placed on the upper part of the tablet.

The Palio of the "Contrade di Siena"

Though we do not know much about the origins of the Palio of Siena, it is certain that this feast, the most popular and famous one of the town, existed already in 1310, when a document of the General Council of Siena officially instituted the Palio to be run on August 16th in honour of the Blessed Virgin. Originally the Palio which took place in the middle of August was only the crowning of a popular feast, after the battle of Monteaperti in 1260, with the victory of the Sienese people over the Florentines, it became ever more important and had a political meaning. In fact, by offering candles, they wished to honour the Madonna, to whom the people of Siena had consacrated themselves, and at the same time to confirm the autonomy and indipendence of the Free Town. Only in 1656 a second Palio, the « Palio of the Contrade », which takes place on July 2, in honour of the Madonna of Provenzano, was officially approved. The Sienese Contrade (districts) are practically the result of the decline of the central government in the Middle Ages. This situation brought people to rule themselves and join various associations. In the 13th century the Contrade were about 80, but gradually their number decreased and now they are only 17. Today the Contrade do not have only a representative function and their activity does not end with the Palio. Rather, we can say that in the present feverish world their vitality has a particular significance. Each Sienese is so tied to his contrada that we can say that the individual lives for the community and the community takes care of the individual specially on the most important occasions of his life. The life of the Contrada is very intense for twelve months, but specially during the days of the Palio, when a suggestive feast has to be prepared. As a matter of fact, the Palio is more than a simple folk show or a historical celebration in costumes. Today as yesterday the Palio is the feast of Siena and Its 17 contrade, which fight for the painted silk drape. It is practically a rite, in which Siena since the drawing of lots, four weeks before the race up to the moment when the horses enter the arena for the final crazy race, shows its true face and relives with enthusiasm and nostalgic passion a wonderful dream of a splendid past. The crazy race lasts only a moment and is the most exciting part of the Palio. It is preceded by the picturesque parade, which coming from the courtyard of the Government Palace, in the Cathedral quare, enters the Campo, transformed for this occasion into a arena, which is unique of its kind. The Parade, animated by the splendid costumes and the sound of drums and the surprising flag waving, moves slowly along the track. It is an incomparable commemoration of the life and greatness of the ancient Republic. And Siena could not offer a more suggestive and proper scenery for it.

The Palio of the "Contrade di Siena"

The Major Page of the Contrada of the Lupa

The Leader of the Contrada of the Civetta

The Historical Parade opens with six mace-bearers and the flag-bearer of the Municipality, on horse-back with the white and black flag, called the "Balzana", which is the emblem of Siena. After the trumpeters and the musicians of the Palace, come the flag-bearers of the Towns, Lands and Castels which formed once the State of Siena; then the flag-bearer and the three Magistrates of Merchandise and the representatives of the major arts. Then come the "comparse" of the ten contrade which run, all in the colourful costumes of their contrade; they are a drum-bearer, two ensigns, a captain, four pages, a flag-bearer, a jockey on horse-back and the so called "barbaresco" who leads tho race-horse. After the ten "comparse" of the seven contrade which do not run and the Captain of Justice, comes the Triumphal Chariot which, richly painted, bears the Palio which the winning contrada will receive as a prize, the white and black "balzana" and a small bell, called "Martinella". Even the horse-men of the six contrade which now do not exist, take part in the Parade.

The Major Page of the Contrada of the Valdimontone

The Major Page of the Contrada of the Tartuca

Views of the Palio of Siena

The Cathedral adorned with the flags of the 17 *Contrade* (districts of Siena) for the Palio, which is held on the feast of the Assumption on 16 August. For the earlier Palio held on the 2 July, on the other hand, the religious celebrations are held in the church of Santa Maria di Provenzano. Below: the Triumphal Cart which closes the Historic Procession.

Siena's Palazzo Pubblico decked with flags, and the blessing of the horse and jockey in the Oratory of the Contrada in the afternoon before the race.

The Centurion of the "Terzi" (the tripartite division of the city) in his picturesque red costume.
The Dinner of the General Trial of one of the civic districts, the *Contrada dell'Oca*. The event is an important one for the Sienese who celebrate it, in a kind of collective rite, by gathering in the main street or piazza of the Contrada. Below: the fantastic general view of the Campo from on top of the tall tower of the Palazzo Pubblico during the Historic Procession.

The Palio: the horserace and the Victory Dinner

And here in the photos on this page are some shots of the concluding phases of the Palio. The start of the race: the starting-rope in about to fall and the horses, mounted by their jockeys dressed in a simple habit with the colours of their *Contrada* (district), paw the ground waiting for the "off".

They're off: the horses are launched on their hurtling and dramatic race round the Campo for the conquest of the Palio.

It is an enthralling and unpredictable spectacle which arouses bursts of tremendous enthusiasm among the huge crowd of spectators: fresh hopes and ancient passions are revived, and the real and deep-seated spirit of the different *Contrade* is laid bare.

And if the enthusiasm of the crowd is indescribable during the race, even more so is the joy of the supporters of the victorious *Contrada*: after an exultant Te Deum of thanksgiving in the Church of the Madonna of Provenzano on 2 July or in the Cathedral on 16 August, they will bear the Palio (banner) in triumph through the streets of the city amid the beating of drums, the pealing of church bells and the exuberant waving of flags. The winning of the Palio is the occasion for rejoicing, and the inhabitants of the victorious *Contrada* conclude the celebrations with a splendid Dinner of Victory.

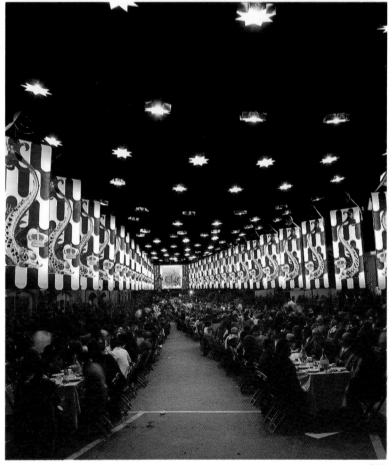

The Castles and hills of Chianti

The Chianti area is reached from Siena by way of the Via Chiantigiana. By taking this beautiful panoramic road that dominates the valley, in a few minutes we reach the centre of this territory where the testimonies of history, art and nature which have made it what it is are clearly evident. Not only does the land speak for itself, but the distinctive, brighly-coloured billboards at the side of the roads with the slogan "Siete nel mondo del Gallo Nero" (You're in the world of the Black Cockerel) announce to the tourist that he is in the land of Chianti Classico (for the emblem of the Black Cockerel distinguishes the necks of bottles of that typically Tuscan wine).

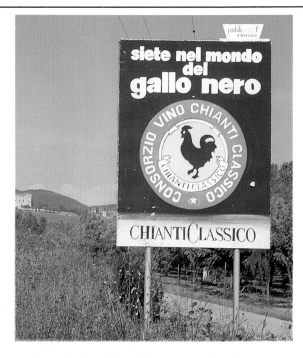

Situated between the provinces of Siena and Florence, the Chianti territory covers some 70,000 hectares, and has a harmonious, feudal appearance. The landscape it offers its visitors is still intact, a paradise of former times in which pollution and cement are unknown. Half of the territory is woodland, and the other half is cultivated with vines, olive-groves and other crops. The territory's altitude varies between 200 and 600 metres above sea-level.

These rolling hills are dotted with rustic farmhouses, historic fortified villages, castles, towers, abbeys and ancient parish churches. The revolving seasons each have their particular smells and particular fascination. But autumn is especially magical, with its warm soft tones and its landscape variegated with splashes of red and yellow.

The etymology of the word Chianti is disputed: it may derive from "Clango" (sounds of the horn), or from the Etruscan "Clante-i". What is certain, given the many fossil remains of vines at San Vivaldo and the provenance of many Etruscan drinking-vessels from the area, is that it was inhabited by the Etruscans, who were perhaps the first to plant vines in the territory. Wine was certainly being produced here in Etruscan and Roman times. But the first written documents testifying to viticulture date to 913 (church of Santa Cristina at Lucignano) and 1037 (Badia Coltibuono).

The word Chianti, referred to the geographic zone, appears for the first time on a vellum charter dating to 1100 in the archive of Badia Coltibuono. But the word was only extended to the local wine from 1384, when a statute was issued by the league of Chianti, founded by the Communes of Radda, Gaiole and Castellina (and later Greve) for administrative and military purposes in 1250.

This league was interrupted by the Grand-Duke of Tuscany in 1700, but was revived in 1924, when many farms in the area banded themselves together into a Consortium for the defence of their wine, which they called Chianti Classico, with the characteristic symbol or device of the Black Cockerel which continues to distinguish Chianti Classico today.

At the present time there are some 250 wine-growing farms in the territory dedicated to the production and marketing of Chianti. In recent years, many of them have promoted — as a sideline — tourist development by providing holiday accommodation and other leisure facilities.

This land, which represents the heart of Tuscany and its image in the world, was of great importance in Roman times: in fact it was a vital area of communication between Rome and her Empire to the north, thanks to the major thoroughfares of the Via Cassia and the Via Francigena.

In the Middle Ages it was long a bone of contention between Ghibelline (pro-imperial) Siena and Guelph (pro-papal) Florence: its fortified settlements and castles aligned themselves now on the one side, now on the other, according to the military force and strategic positions of the moment. Some noble families threw in their lot with the Florentines (Ricasoli, Guidi, Firidolfi), others with the Sienese (Berardenghi). Of five centuries of war it will suffice to mention the Battle of Monteaperti (1260), when the Florentines were routed by the Sienese, causing Dante (in his Inferno) to bemoan "the havoc and the great slaughter which dyed the Arbia red". In 1555 Florence imposed her rule over most of Tuscany, and the end of the internecine strife also signalled a change in architecture: buildings were developed horizontally, defensive towers were abandoned, and the aristocracy began to build build large and magnificent villas for themselves outside the town walls. The first isolated farmhouses also began to appear.

After a period of decline due to the depopulation of the territory, there has been a recovery in the last thirty years with the arrival of new settlers first from England, then from Switzerland, Holland and France, and most recently from Germany, who together with the remaining ancient families have begun a process of regeneration which is still undergoing a period of growth today. This development is especially due to the production of wine, which was proclaimed a "Wine of protected denomination and origin" (i.e. appellation contrôlée) by the Grand-Duke of Tuscany, Pietro Leopoldo, as early as 1716, and is now famous throughout the world.

In the mid-18th century the introduction of a new vessel for Chianti, the famous "fiasco" (flask), led to a growth in its consumption and was almost to become a symbol of it. But it was not until 1870 that an official formula for the production of Chianti Classico was issued: this was when Bettino Ricasoli (1808-1890), founder of the modern oenology of Chianti, codified the proper mixture for his wine as follows: 70 percent Sangiovese, the grape which gives body and colour; 20 percent Canaiolo, which confers fragrance and softness; and 10 percent Trebbiano and Malvasia, which add a slight touch of acidity and sharpness. At that time, the grapes, after being picked and placed in vats, were pressed for three-to-four days until the dregs had well settled. After a period of rest for about twenty days, the wine was removed from the vats and placed in barrels in which it was subjected to the process known as "governo" or refermentation by adding small quantities of selected grapes previously dried on reed mats.

Also worth mentioning is the local "Vinsanto" (sweet white raisin wine). This is obtained with white grapes (Trebbiano and Malvasia) dried on trellises, made into wine after 3/4 months by pressing them through sieves after having picked them from the bunch to separate them from impurities, and then aged for four years in small barrels (known as "caratelli") placed in airy wine-cellars. Apart from its production of wine, the Chianti country is also distinguished for its production of extra virgin olive oil, which a recent article in the New York Times adjudicated one of the ten best in the world.

But to enable the tourist to gain a better knowledge of this small territory of the province of Siena, we will describe below a practical itinerary, starting out from the southern area, and listing the most important localities and monuments, of which we will give a succinct historical and artistic description.

Sangiovese Grapes   *Trebbiano Toscano Grapes*

The Castles and hills of Chianti

Castelnuovo Berardenga is a small wine-producing centre where once stood the "Castello Nuovo": the castle from which it derives its name, and which was built by the Republic of Siena in 1366. Only a few traces of it now remain, hidden inside the Villa Chigi-Saracini, an imposing building surrounded by a beautiful wooded park.

We are now in the southernmost district of Chianti, and only a part of its territory forms part of the Chianti Classico zone proper. Leaving Castelnuovo Berardegna, we now enter the "world of the Black Cockerel" — homeland of Chianti Classico — and, after passing the first wine-producer on the road (the farm of Felsina), we continue to San Gusmé: entering the Sienese gateway, we immediately have the impression of being in a fortified settlement with narrow streets and a miniature piazza.

Turning back by the way we came, we come to Villa a Sesta: the little town preserves no traces of its historic past. But worth noticing is the Castello di Sestaccia on a nearby hill; its ruins still testify to its grandeur in former times.

In its environs, by taking unmetalled roads, we can visit the 18th century Villa d'Arceno, with a huge park containing an artificial lake; Castel in Villa, former castle of the Villa Guistrigona whose keep still retains its medieval appearance; the Villa la Pagliaia and the vineyards of the Fattoria dei Pagliaresi, descendents of the Counts of Berardenga. Here is visible, to one side of the villa, the ancient 13th century fortified tower.

We also recommend a visit to the Castello di Bossi, whose history is inseparably linked with the Berardenghi family, and which suffered serious damage at the hands of the Florentines led by the rival Ricasoli family. The existing structure dates to the 15th century, but incorporates the 12th century keep. The fortress played a key role at the time of the battle of Monteaperti, situated as it is close to the site of the battle. It was later in large part demolished, and the building assumed its present appearance, with the villa built over the glacis of the ancient castle and opening out into a large courtyard, a feature presented by many villas in the area and designed to facilitate the entry and exit of carriages.

From here we continue to San Felice, a fortified medieval settlement expertly restored during the last fifteen years and retaining an aura of great fascination. Though it has experienced periods of abandonment, it is now enjoying a revival, and the wine-producer that owns it is one of the most -up-to-date and best-equipped in the area; a large range of high-quality wines and other produce is on sale. Facing onto the piazza are the Chapel and Manor-House which contains a magnificent wine-press.

San Gusmé: panoramic view

An ancient Grapes press preserved in a farm at San Felice

The Castle of Brolio

Not far away, situated on an isolated hill, is Brolio, a name of Lombard origin signifying a wooded place, with the residence of its Lord at the centre. The Castle of Brolio, synonimous with the Ricasoli family, can be visited every day in the year. It is approached through a single entrance, once a drawbridge. It is undoubtedly one of the most famous places in the Chianti area, with a long history and many legends behind it. It even has a resident ghost: a lone baron, the Barone di Ferro, dressed in back, is said to wander on horseback through the Castle's domains on stormy nights.

Of ancient origin (9th century), the Castle stands on an isolated hill to the south of the Chianti area, and commands extensive panoramic views over the surrounding landscape. It was a powerful Florentine bulwark, reconstructed in the 15th century after having been destroyed by the Aragonese in 1478, with the addition of a massive circuit of walls, reinforced at the corners by impregnable bastions.

The Castle always represented a thorn in the flesh of the Sienese Republic. By order of Siena it was completely demolished, but was reconstructed by the Florentines for Piergiovanni Ricasoli and completed in 1553. The building we see today, however, dates largely to the seconf half of the 19th century; of the ancient medieval structure the earthworks, the keep, the Chapel of San Jacopo, the sentry's covered walks and the cellars. In its vicinity Etruscan remains have also been found.

The Castle is today the site of one of the most important wine-producing centres of the Chianti area, with extensive wine-cellars and Manor House (Palazzo Padronale).

Castle of Brolio: panoramic view and main façade of the Castle

The Castle of Cacchiano, Tornano and Meleto

Before arriving in Gaiole in Chianti, we may stop to visit the Castle of Cacchiano, which seems to have been built over the remains of a Roman settlement and is now completely transformed into a villa. Not far away is the Castle of Tornano, of which the majestic tower and an adjacent building, recently restored, remain intact. In the same area, situated on top of a high, partly wooded hill, is the Castle of Meleto, one of the most important fortifications of the medieval League of Chianti. Its 13th century tower is now incorporated at the centre of the existing building, which it exceeds in height. A stretch of the medieval ramparts is also visible. The two angular towers on the east side were added in c. 1500.

In 1738 part of the Castle was converted into a manor house at the centre of estates famous for the quality of their wine. Here the landscaping of the slopes into terraces and artificial embankments increased substantially in the last century in response to the demands of agronomists and hydraulic experts to adapt the land to cultivation and to facilitate the drainage and stability of the slopes.

Nearby is the settlement of Castagnoli, another fortified hill-top centre: its main nucleus is well-preserved, a typical example of a manorial settlement enclosed by a defensive circuit of walls, though this unfortunately remains intact only in part.

The Castle of Cacchiano, view of the Castle's Tornano and the Castel Meleto with its towers.

Santa Maria di Spaltenna, the Castle and Barbischio

And so we arrive in Gaiole in Chianti, whose territory is wholly comprised in the Chianti Classico zone. A small fortified settlement situated on the valley floor of the Massellone torrent (to the west stands the ancient castle, now converted into a hotel, and the 12th century romanesque parish church of Santa Maria a Spaltenna), it has since time immemorial been a market for the trading of goods, animals and the produce of the land. Its name appears for the first time in a donation to the Badia (abbey) of Poggibonsi in 998. It seems that its first inhabitants came from Barbischio, a picturesque fortified settlement situated on top of a wooded hill to the east of Gaiole. Of its fortifications demolished in 1530 little remains; but the 11th century tower of the keep, entirely restored, is still proudly extant. In the environs of Gaiole is Vertine, which is mentioned in the historical sources from 1049 on. Surrounded by a fine circuit of walls, this little fortified settlements comprises many well-preserved 13th century houses, dominated by a massive tower and the keep of the ancient castle.

Continuing our itinerary, we come to San Donato in Perano. Here we find a 17th century villa which has absorbed the remains of the medieval fortifications. Its tallest part is also its most ancient. The fine 16th century portal of the Chapel may be noted in the façade.

The church of Santa Maria in Spaltenna, the Castle of Spaltenna and a panoramic view of the fortified settlement of Barbischio

The Abbey of Coltibuono and Pieve Asciata

As the last stage of our itinerary, we ascend to Badia a Coltibuono (600 m.), a complex consisting of an Abbey, a wine-producing farm and a restaurant. It is certain that the friars of the Vallombrosan Order cultivated vines and olives here since 1100. The Abbey, dating to 1049, is a fine example of romanesque architecture, with a Latin-cross plan and a dome resting on an octagonal base over the crossing. To its left is the bell-tower dating to 1160; to its right the monastery (c. 1800) now converted into a residence.
Etruscan excavations have been carried out in its vicinity, on the Poggio di Cetamura.

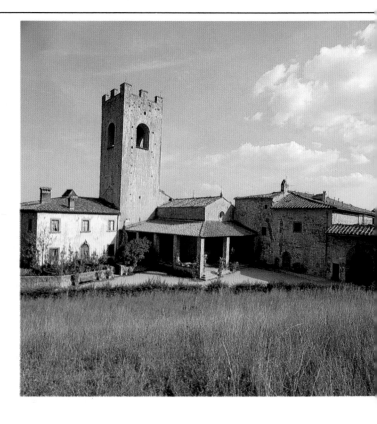

The Abbey of Coltibuono and a panoramic view of Pieve Asciata

Also in the southern part of the Sienese Chianti area we find the village of Pianella, beyond which we once again enter the "World of the Black Cockerel": land of Chianti Classico. A short distance ahead, by making a small detour to the right, we may visit San Giusto a Rentennano. Here we find a Renaissance villa built over the fortress of the Ricasoli, which was destroyed by the Sienese in 1390: it was on that occasion that gunpowder was used for the first time in Tuscany. In its vicinity, a further detour may be recommended to those who like to discover the most hidden and uncontaminated corners of this rural paradise: a visit, namely, to the Canonica of Cerreto, a well-preserved romanesque church with a single nave and bell-tower.

In its vicinity the remains of the Castle of Cerreto can be glimpsed amid dense woodland; only some stretches of wall and the ruins of a tower remain.
We then come to Pieve Asciata, a fortified church with a fine bell-tower. From here we continue to Selvole. Of its ancient castle we can see only some stretches of its bastions and ramparts, as well as an imposing keep which has been restored; though truncated, it must once have been a fortification of great importance.

San Polo in Rosso, grape-harwest in the Chianti country

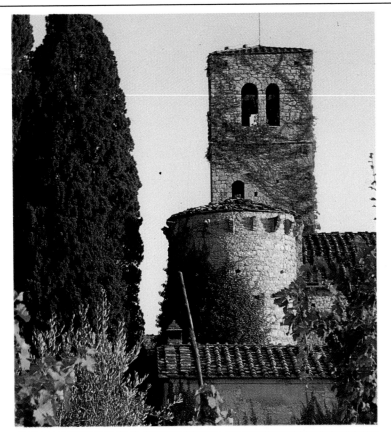

Over the ruins of the Castle was erected the villa of the Malavolti family, a fine example of late 18th century Sienese architecture, with interior decorations of great interest. The ancient Oratory of San Martino, with a 16th century portal, is also of considerable interest.

A short distance further ahead is San Sano. This is a characteristic agricultural centre huddled round the small parish church. The monument to a frog ("Rana Beona") is curious.

We continue to Lecchi where we can see the Castello di Monteluco a Lecchi, which belonged for centuries — like many other castles — to the powerful Ricasoli family. It has recently undergone a questionable restoration. In the past, in view of its dominant strategic position, it was frequently involved in the wars between Siena and Florence. Worth noting in the same ares in the romanesque church of San Martino.

We now continue in the direction of Radda and soon come to two wonderful sights: the first in Castello di Ama, a stronghold of Etruscan origin which is mentioned for the first time as a hamlet in 998. During the prolonged war between the Sienese and the Florentines, it suffered repeated invasions, causing grave damage to its buildings. Of the ancient castle no trace remains: it was demolished by the Aragonese in the 15th century. Its recovery was slow, and only in the late 17th and early 18th century were the Villa Pianigiani and Villa Riccucci built over the ruins of the castle, completely altering the settlement's appearance.

The second notable monument we come to on the road to Radda is one of the most magnificent fortified parish churches in the Chianti country: San Polo in Rosso. It too was the property of the Ricasoli and suffered all the vicissitudes to which the history of the area was subject, including a siege by the Aragonese to whom it surrendered. Returning to Florentine control, its fortifications were reinforced. During the present century, major restorations were carried out by the Ricasoli, including the construction of a balcony over the main façade, and a stone-built ancillary building, used as a farmhouse.

Just before reaching Radda we can make a brief visit to the parish church of San Giusto in Salcio.

A picturesque view of San Polo in Rosso and peasant at work during the grape-harvest

Radda in Chianti and Castle of Volpaia

Radda in Chianti, situated on a hill-top at an altitude of 530 m., together with its surrounding territory forms part of the Chianti Classico area. It still retains its medieval town-plan, radiating outwards from its centre: the ancient parish church of San Niccolò around which the town is huddled.

Capital of the League of Chianti since 1415, whose banners bore the heraldic device of the Black Cockerel, which is now the trade-mark of Chianti Classico, Radda in Chianti was the seat of the podestà (chief magistrate) with jurisdiction over the three districts of Radda, Gaiole and Castellina. Located on the confines of Florentine territory, the Castle of Radda was often involved in the protracted and sometimes bloody hostilities between Florence and its rival Siena: it was damaged for the first time by the Sienese in 1268, and occupied by Charles of Anjou in 1478. All that remains of it today are some stretches of rampart and the ruins of towers. The 15th century Palazzo del Podestà, seat of the medieval government and now the Town Hall, has an important fresco of the Florentine school in its atrium. Just outside the little town is situated a Franciscan Monastery, built in a late-Gothic style, with a 16th century portal. A scenic walk leads under the western walls of the town, from where magnificent views can be enjoyed over the valley and the surrounding hills clad in vineyards and woods. Radda's economy is today mainly based on the production and marketing of wine and incipient tourism. Worth visiting, to the north of Radda, almost on the slopes of Monte Querciabella, is Volpaia on account of its medieval castle. Dating back to the 10th century, the Castle has an elliptical plan, and is still pervaded by a sombre medieval atmosphere.

There are many medieval buildings, including the church of Volpaia and especially the Commenda (benefice) of Sant'Eufrosino, which is now used for exhibitions and other cultural events. Below it is a wine-cellar in which the famous wine of the hills of Radda is aged.

Radda in Chianti: the tower over the southern wall and the main façade of the Castle of Volpaia

Villa Vistarenni and the Certosa di Pontignano

Also in the vicinity of Radda is the magnificent 16th century Villa Vistarenni, built by the Strozzi family. The locality is mentioned as early as the 11th century. Also well worthwhile is a visit to "Il Piccolo Museo del Chianti" at Montevertine: a small museum containing a fascinating collection of tools, implements and household objects which vividly conjure up a picture of the area's traditional rural society in the past. Nearby is the National Park of Cavriglia, a delight for children, in which many animals are kept in a state of semi-liberty.

Returning in our tracks, we now take the Vagliagli road, a route that passes close to the springs of the Arbia, through a characteristic and poetic landscape. From here we reach the Villa dell'Aiola, situated over an embankment supported by a system of fortifications surrounded by broad moats. The state of conservation is excellent and gives some indication of what an imposing castle it must have been.

View of the façade of the Villa Vistarenni

Of the four original towers two still remain. These and the surviving ramparts represent, in size and impressiveness, one of the most interesting examples of fortifications in the Chianti area.

Before continuing our itinerary beyond Vagliagli, an interesting agricultural settlement, we recommend a visit to the Certosa (charterhouse) of Pontignano. This was founded in 1342, and underwent alterations and enlargements in the 17th century, with the addition of the Large Cloisters. The interior of the church is decorated with fine frescoes, below which are some fine carved and inlaid choir-stalls of the 16th century. Francesco Vanni's Crucifixion over the high altar is striking. Acquired by the University of Siena, the Certosa is now the seat of the Mario Bracci University College (providing accommodation for many students). The characteristic "Feast of the New Moon" is celebrated at Pontignano on the first Sunday in July each year.

The corridor and Large Cloisters in the Certosa of Pontignano

Fonterutoli, San Leonino and the Fortress of Castellina

Following the Via Chiantigiana, main highway of the Chianti area, we pass through Querciagrossa, where the great 15th century sculptor Jacopo della Quercia was born; his best known works include the "Fonte Gaia" in the Campo at Siena. We may stop here a moment to see the remains of a castle situated on the left just before leaving the little town.

Before arriving in Castellina in Chianti we come to Fonterutoli, an ancient Etrusco-Roman settlement. A number of Etruscan tombs have been found in its vicinity, while a few traces of paving on the site date to the Roman period. The existing farmhouse on the site has belonged to the same family since 1435, and its present owner, Lapo Mazzei, is currently chairman of the Consortium of the Black Cockerel (the trade association for the protection of Chianti Classico). Facing onto the little piazza are a church and a number of buildings in brick of great elegance.

We continue along the Via Chiantigiana until we come to the intersection on the left for San Leonino. This ancient fortified settlement is worth a little detour. Its monuments include the ancient parish church of San Leonino in Conio and the Castle which still preserves its medieval appearance.

Continuing along the Via Chiantigiana, we continue to climb until we reach Castellina in Chianti (578 m.), one of the highest towns in the area. Situated in a dominant position on top of a hill between the valleys of the Arbia, Elsa and Pesa, it commands sweeping views over a rolling landscape of arable land, olive groves, vineyards and oak woods. In the Middle Ages a feud of the nobles of Trebbio, it later became a fortified village under Florentine rule at the beginning of the 15th century. The Florentines surrounded it with a circuit of walls, and turned it into one of their main defensive bulwarks against Siena.

Attacked by the Sienese on several occasions, and occupied by them in 1478, Castellina only found peace with the end of the war in 1555. The town still retains part of its defensive system, such as the characteristic covered sentry's walk along the Via delle Volte, with narrow machicolations from which charming views of the landscape can be enjoyed, and the Rocca (fortress), a massive construction with a 14th century tower and 15th century keep which stands at the centre of the town. Restored in 1927, it is now the Town Hall. The origins of the area are of great antiquity: in fact an Etruscan tomb of the 6th century B.C., discovered in 1507, can be seen not far from the town, in the locality of Montecalvario. A stroll along the main street of Castellina is recommended; it is flanked by handsome, well-maintained town-houses built over the remains of older houses. Especially striking is the 16th century Palazzo Ugolini with a long façade rusticated in its lower storey. Unfortunately the two town-gates are no longer exstant; the Florentine one was demolished after the war because in a dangerous condition.

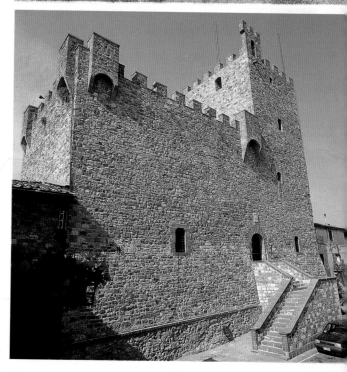

Panoramic view of Fonterutoli, San Leonino and the Fortress of Castellina in Chianti

The Farm-house "Rocca delle Macíe"

Worth noting in the environs of Castellina, close to Casalecchi, is one of the oldest romanesque buildings in the Chianti country: the Badiola or Santa Maria al Colle. It was in this locality that the Castle of Trebbio, demolished by the Sienese army in the 15th century, is thought to have been situated. Continuing our route along the Via Chiantigiana, we reach (by a brief detour) Pietrafitta. Its castle was destroyed by the Aragonese and the Sienese during the siege of Castellina. All that remain today are the handsome tower, the walls that enclose the few houses (mainly restored), and the church reconstructed in 1940. Also worth visiting in the vicinity of Castellina in Chianti are the charming village of Ricavo, in the direction of San Donato in Poggio, and S. Agnese, on the road leading down to Poggibonsi. The latter is a romanesque church already mentioned in documents in 1056, of which only the right wall and part of the bell-tower remain. Returning towards Siena, we now take the road for Castellina Scalo, along which we may visit Villa Leccia, where some stretches of wall can still be glimpsed and which must once have marked the site of a fortified settlement.

The dispersed settlement, with the houses in the midst or on the margins of the estates, is a characteristic aspect of the landscape of the Chianti area, at one time largely farmed on a share-cropping system. Yet the functional position of the farm-house did not ignore or disdain the search for a beautiful site, preferably on high ground, surrounded by or preceded by a fine avenue of cypresses. Moreover, the modernization of agriculture has here tended to privilege the most remunerative crops, especially viticulture. Today, indeed, an increasingly frequent sight is that of large specialized vineyards, whose geometrically aligned rows of vines do not disturb the essential harmony of the landscape and harmonize well with the older farms. One model farm that we pass on the road down to Castellina Scalo is that of Rocca della Maciè, a mainly viticultural farm established in a brand-new farm complex faithfully reconstructed on the model of ancient medieval settlements: a typical example of how modernized farming can be practised in full respect for the culture and environment of the Chianti area.

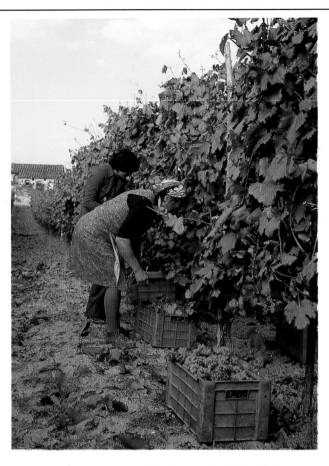

Grape-harvest, a view of the Rocca delle Macìe farm and a wine -cellar for the ageing of wine in the Chianti country

Lilliano, Villa Cerna and Monteriggioni

This is followed by Lilliano with its formhouse and the parish church of Santa Cristina, of which only the façade with its portal survives of the original romanesque building, while the handsome bell-tower dates to the 17th century.

Of the ancient castle and the fortified settlement that once stood here, no trace remains. In its vicinity, situated on a small hill surrounded by vineyards, is the Villa Cerna, built over the ancient church of the Santi Donato e Cesareo of which the two bell-towers remain. The villa itself is handsome. On a hill facing it stands the Castello di Rencine, a modest building with a fine garden and an adjacent formhouse, although a fortress magnificently surrounded by ramparts and towers reportedly once stood on the site.

Leaving the "World of the Black Cockerel", we come (just beyond Castellina Scalo on the road for Siena) to Monteriggioni, a very distinctive medieval fortified settlement erected on top of a small hill. It was built by the Sienese in the early years of the 13th century as a defensive bulwark and surrounded by an imposing circuit of walls (570 m. in circumference), fortified with 14 well-preserved towers. The fascination of Monteriggioni is unique, both from inside, viewed from the piazza where a famous blacksmith — one of the most long-established in Italy — still works today, and from outside, especially by night when the walls are lit up picturesquely by artificial light.

Picturesque view of Lilliano, the façade of the Villa Cerna and a panoramic shot of the walls of Monteriggioni

As already mentioned, vines were cultivated, and wine produced, in the Chianti area as early as Etruscan and Roman times. In more recent times, we find the quality of Chianti wine scrupulously defended in various documents, such as that issued by Grand-Duke Pietro Leopoldo in 1716. Moreover, in the wine-cellars of some castles, or those of the older farms, it is still possible to find equipment at least three centuries old for the making of wine, such as the wine-press, a barrel, a period cart or a millstone.

We have now finished our journey through the territory of Chianti. From any hilltop during our itinerary, in a moment of rest or reflection, we can stop to admire once again this singular landscape of gently rolling hills entirely shaped by the millennial work of man. The symbiosis between man and the environment is total. An eloquent witness to this harmony between man and nature is afforded not only by the landscape itself, but also by Ambrogio Lorenzetti's famous fresco in Siena depicting "Good Government in the Countryside": here, from the walls of the city, one could look out over a territory densely cultivated with vines, olives and wheat, a prospect which surely did not idealize the daily life of the 14th century, just as the landscape we see today is no less surely the product of the 20th century.

Ancient work tools, and an evocative panoramic view of the hills of Chianti

CONTENTS

L. 12.000
I.V.A. INCLUSA